ROGER WILLIAMS

ROGER WILLIAMS
HIS LIFE, WORK, and IDEALS

By

Charles Smull Longacre, M.A.

Author of "Freedom—Civil and Religious," "The Church in Politics," "Studies in the Fundamentals of Civil and Religious Liberty and of Civil Government." Editor for twenty-eight years of LIBERTY, the magazine of religious freedom, published in Washington, D.C. General Secretary of the International Religious Liberty Association for twenty-eight years.

Illustrations by Robert M. Eldridge

Review and Herald Publishing Association
Takoma Park, Washington, D.C.
PRINTED IN U.S.A.

DEDICATED TO THE CAUSE

OF CIVIL AND RELIGIOUS

LIBERTY

Contents

Illustrations

Roger Williams in Childhood

Roger Williams was born in Wales about the beginning of the seventeenth century. His father established a merchant-tailor shop in London, where young Roger worked in his childhood, assisting his father in the business. His London home was near Newgate prison and only a short space from the Smithfield Plaza, where many of the so-called heretics were burned at the stake, or "hung by the neck" until they were dead. These executions were frequent in the childhood days of young Williams. His sympathies were stirred as he witnessed these executions for conscience' sake, and he developed a spirit of independent inquiry and a feeling of abhorrence against religious persecution. From childhood he was considered a rebel against the established church order.

Preface

This book has been especially written to meet an imperative need. No man ever had a clearer vision of the proper relationship of church and state, of the fallacies and dangers of a totalitarian or authoritarian system of government—that is, one that rules all men in all things, both secular and spiritual—than did Roger Williams.

In the United States it has been taken for granted that since the founders of the American Republic placed a Bill of Rights in the Federal Constitution, the liberties of American citizens are forever secure, and that the proper relationship of church and state has been finally and forever settled. Unfortunately, such is not the case. Wherever we look, outside of America as well as in America, the inalienable rights of man are being more and more regulated and restricted, and nearly all the activities

of life, in both the spiritual and the secular realm,
are being regimented and circumscribed. In every
country the question of the relation of church and
state holds the center of the stage. Everywhere the
nations are beginning to set limits to freedom of
action, and many are setting up the authority of
the state as supreme in all things, both religious
and civil.

Roger Williams lived in times when church
and state were united both in Europe and in America; and in certain parts of the world the church
was in supreme control both spiritually and po-
litically. In his day, it was considered heretical,
seditious, and treasonable to advocate and work
for the separation of church and state, not only in
Europe, but in the Puritan colonies of America.
The advocacy of this doctrine led to the banishment of Roger Williams and to the founding of a
new and independent government in Rhode Island,
which incorporated the ideals of its founder, and
granted to each individual, for the first time in
history, the full enjoyment of his inalienable rights,
and complete civil and religious liberty in matters
of faith and conscience.

The famous debate between Roger Williams
and John Cotton, which was published in a book
entitled, "The Bloudy Tenent of Persecution," is
in its main features set forth in one of the chapters
of this book. There are only two of the original
copies of "The Bloudy Tenent of Persecution"

preserved, so far as present records indicate. The principles set forth in this book by Roger Williams need to be reiterated. No one ever stated the fundamental principles of civil and religious liberty more clearly than did he. No thoughtful observer can fail to see the sinister trends away from liberty. Unless this tendency is checked by public sentiment, the heritage of civil and religious liberty is doomed for the future. An adherence and a devotion to the great ideals which laid the foundation of the greatest republic in the world, will also lead to the preservation of the principles upon which the perpetuity of that Republic, as well as other republics, now rests.

Roger Williams was the apostle of a doctrine which in time became the fundamental tenet of American philosophy of civil government—the proposition that the civil authorities have no jurisdiction over the conscience in religious matters, and that the civil government is divinely ordained to function "in civil things only."

Because of the courage which he manifested when it was treasonable to express his convictions on the subject of the freedom of the soul in spiritual matters, he won for himself a place in the Hall of Fame, and in the hearts of all men who love freedom more than slavery. Whatever rights to untrammeled thought and action the people enjoy in human government, they possess largely as a result of the matchless teachings of this remarkable man who caught a vision of the divine prerogative of the individual to enjoy his God-given rights.

Williams was fortunate to possess a personality that was winning and a spiritual integrity which would not compromise with expediency. The reason he was not bound to a stake and burned as were a host of other martyrs of his day, and other days, was that he succeeded in making his escape from the snare of the spiritual fowlers, in a land where it was possible to flee to a place of safety. But even if he had perished before the realization of his dream of a "free church in a free state," the ideal which he advocated and the seeds of soul liberty which he planted in the hearts of Americans, would have survived. That is the proof of the value and importance of the principles which he advocated, and which are quite fully set forth in this work. They are imperishable principles because they represent the basic philosophy of the ideals of God in the ordination of human government.

The author, who has spent the best years of his life in defense of the principles of civil and religious liberty, not only in America, but in other countries, commends the first great American champion of religious liberty, Roger Williams, and his ideals, to the general public, "that government of the people, by the people, and for the people shall not perish from the earth."

THE AUTHOR

Roger Williams: Builder of a Republic

Roger Williams and the ideals and fundamental principles which he advocated in the establishment of a new government in America, have not received the study and attention which they deserve. Amid scorn, persecution, and banishment, he held steadfast to his ideals, and was determined to found, in the American wilderness, a new republic in which church and state would be completely separated and in which each individual would enjoy absolute freedom of conscience in all religious matters. As the Honorable Augusta W. Hinshaw says: "Perhaps much more than we have realized, he became the practical founder of the new republic which remains as lively an experiment today as when the young believer in a separate church and state began the policy of Providence."

A frequent recurrence to fundamental principles is absolutely necessary for the preservation of our precious heritage of liberty. It is a well-known axiom that a truth neglected is a truth lost. Democracy and human liberty cannot be maintained on any other basis than the complete separation of church and state as advocated by Roger Williams. For these paramount reasons the author of this work feels that he can render no greater service to the cause of democracy and human liberty than to restate a few of the great fundamental principles and ideals of civil government and its rightful functions, as advocated by this great apostle of soul liberty. In these times, when human rights are treated as pawns on the chessboard by human governments, when every activity of life is regulated, restricted, and regimented, irrespective of constitutional guaranties to the contrary, it becomes doubly incumbent upon the citizenry to familiarize themselves with the principles and the struggle which in the beginning brought about the establishment of democracy and human rights, and resulted in the separation of church and state that each might function separately and independently in its own sphere.

Our only safety lies in knowing and understanding these fundamental principles, and in defending them at any cost. The inalienable rights of man, whether they be social, political, or economic, must be respected and preserved, no matter what the cost in inconveniences or hardships. And no monetary consideration of mere expediency, no consideration of personal advantage, of utility, race, color, or creed, should ever be permitted to interfere either temporarily or permanently with the supremacy of the soul and the conscience, or with the inviolability of the heritage of inalienable rights, which reside inherently in every human being.

Undoubtedly Sir Edward Coke, and other liberal English statesmen with whom Williams came in contact while serving as secretary and stenographer in the Star Chamber, had a great influence in shaping his ideals of essential justice and democratic principles of civil government; yet it must be recognized that young Williams' mind was greatly agitated and impressed with the Baptist literature that fell into his hands, which set forth the ideals of a free and independent church in a free and independent state. The great fundamental principles of religious liberty advocated by the Baptists made a lasting impress upon him.

Roger Williams, very early in life, came in contact with the Anabaptists, the Mennonites, and the Separatists, all of whom taught that the civil magistrate should not meddle with religious matters, all of whom were opposed to infant baptism, and all of whom suffered the usual civil penalties meted out to religious minorities. The Baptists especially were aggressive, and produced a large amount of religious literature, which they circulated extensively. Evidently young Williams read the confession of faith of the Baptists, published in 1614, in which they declared: "The magistrate is not by virtue of his office to meddle with religion, or matters of conscience, to force or compel men to this or that form of religion, or doctrine; but to leave Christian religion free, to every man's conscience, and to handle only civil transgressions."— *McGlothlin, "Baptist Confession of Faith," p. 82.*

He evidently read a textbook in his day written in 1614, by Leonard Busher, "A Citizen of London," which was presented to King James and the high court of Parliament then sitting, a work entitled, "Religion's Peace, or A Plea for Liberty of Conscience."

"For all good shepherds will divide and separate, and not force, slay, and persecute," Busher declared. "Kings and magistrates are to rule temporal affairs by the swords of their temporal kingdoms, and bishops and ministers are to rule spiritual affairs by the word and Spirit of God, the sword of Christ's spiritual kingdom, and not to intermeddle one with another's authority, office, and function. And it is a great shame for the bishops and ministers not to be able to rule in their church without the assistance of the king and magistrate; yea, it is a great sign they are none of Christ's bishops and ministers. If they were, they would not be afraid nor ashamed of their faith; nor yet would they persuade princes and people to persecute, and force one another to believe them; but would use only the assistance of God's word and Spirit, and therewith suffer their faith and doctrine to be examined, proved, and disputed, both by word and writing."—*"Tracts on Liberty of Conscience," p. 23.*

Another Baptist, John Murton, in 1615, wrote a treatise entitled, "Persecution for Religion Judged and Condemned," and presented it to the king of England, in which many statements like this occur: "No man ought to be persecuted for his religion, be it true or false, so they testify their faithful allegiance to the king." "What authority can any mortal man require more, than of body, goods, life, and all that appertaineth to the outward man? The heart God requireth."—*Id., pp. 95, 108.*

It is evident that Roger Williams, as a student at the Charter House in London, had access to these Baptist works current in his day, because many of these terse sayings of the Baptists occur in many instances in almost the same identical words. He was undoubtedly greatly influenced by these Baptist writings in his early life while he was still an adherent of the popular state church, and they must have made a profound impression upon him and led him finally to the acceptance of the Baptist faith in America.

The early settlers who fled from the persecutions of Old England had resolved to separate church and state in the New World and grant religious freedom to the persecuted of Europe. But the powerful majority soon lost sight of the separation issue in America, and began to persecute the dissenting minorities. Roger Williams espoused the cause of religious minorities and broke connections with his own church, when, to his great sorrow, he discovered that the government of New England and his own church had disavowed only the religious persecutions of Old England, and not the principle of religious persecution. This compelled him to lay aside position, prestige, and preferment a second time, in order that he might make possible in America the establishment of religious liberty as conceived by the Author of Christianity. In the uncharted wilderness he became an exile for his opposition to the established church-and-state order, and he became the founder, not only of a new faith, but of a new Republic, in which the government was of the people and dealt with "civil things only."

The German philosopher and historian Gervinus, in his Introduction to the "History of the Nineteenth Century," says of the principles of religious liberty and the complete separation of church and state as now accepted by the United States and other democratic countries, and first enunciated by the founder of Rhode Island: "In accordance with these principles, Roger Williams insisted, in Massachusetts, upon allowing entire freedom of conscience, and upon entire separation of the church and the state. But he was obliged to flee, and in 1636 he formed in Rhode Island a small and new society in which perfect freedom in matters of faith was allowed and in which the majority ruled in all civil affairs. Here, in a little State, the fundamental principles of political and ecclesiastical liberty practically prevailed, before they were even taught in any of the schools of philosophy in Europe. At that time people predicted only a short existence for these democratical experiments—universal suffrage, universal eligibility to office, the annual change of rulers, perfect religious freedom—the Miltonian doctrines of schisms. But not only have these ideas and these forms of government maintained themselves here, but precisely from this little State have they extended themselves throughout the United States. They have conquered the aristocratic tendencies in Carolina and New York, the High Church in Virginia, the theocracy in Massachusetts, and the monarchy in all America. They have given laws to a continent, and formidable through their moral influence, they lie at the bottom of all the democratic movements which are now shaking the nations of Europe."— *Quoted by Doctor Fish, in "Price of Soul Liberty," pp. 141, 142.*

Roger Williams' little republic in Rhode Island, with its four plantations, became the forerunner of the great American Republic with its forty-eight States. Roger Williams was the first pioneer in America to erect the standard of religious liberty for every person, irrespective of what his religious persuasion might be. He identified himself with that group of Separatists who adopted baptism by immersion upon profession of faith alone, and who consistently, under persecution, advocated the divorcement of religion from the affairs of state. When this separation doctrine was first declared publicly by the Baptists, it was deemed of all doctrines the most pernicious and dangerous. It was to America that the persecuted of Europe fled in the hope that here this doctrine might find root and fertile soil. And it was here that in due time a divine destiny sent Roger Williams, as the apostle of religious liberty and the founder of Rhode Island, to give effective expression to this fundamental principle in governmental institutions.

"Of all the differences between the Old World and the New," says Bryce, "this is perhaps the most salient. Half the wars of Europe, half the internal troubles that have vexed European states, from the Monophysite controversies of the Roman Empire of the fifth century down to the Kulturkampf in the German Empire of the nineteenth, have arisen from theological differences or from the rival claims of church and state."

All the governments of earth were ruled by monarchs who believed they ruled by divine right and that they were absolute in authority in all things both temporal and spiritual. The rulers of the totalitarian governments of today hold to the same beliefs. It is therefore most fitting and profitable that we should study with scrutiny the early struggle in America which was a revolt against the ancient order of things and which ultimately led to the establishment of democracies, the sovereignty of the people, the separation of church and state, and freedom for the individual in religious matters.

The great leaders of the Protestant Reformation did not advocate religious liberty for all men, but for only their own sects. As soon as they became sufficiently powerful and dominant, they formed alliances with the state and recognized the head of the state as empowered to stamp out heretical doctrines. They did not believe that religion could exist or prosper without the aid of the state, or that the stability of government could be maintained without an organic union with the church. The state must have a religion or it would be a godless government. And the church must have the state to correct and punish heretics, or subversive and pernicious religious views and doctrines would threaten the very existence of both church and state. They reasoned, "How could pure religion be maintained if the state did not define it and support it by its authority?" Such reasoning the Protestant Reformers and their successors considered unanswerable logic. In this they did not differ with their Catholic antagonists.

Roger Williams Preaching in Boston

When Roger Williams first arrived in Boston, in 1631, he was invited to preach in the Boston church. He had decided ideas of the relationship that should exist between the church and the civil power, and vigorously advocated them to the Puritan congregation. The Puritans had hoped that the new arrival might serve as their pastor in Boston, but his advocacy of the doctrine of complete separation of church and state not only doomed his chances to preach in Boston, but almost prevented his preaching in any other place in New England. His call to Salem, however, finally was consummated; here he preached for two years. It appeared as if his ideals were doomed not to take root in America.

Roger Williams was the only exception among the Protestant Reformers. When he arrived in America with a commission to act as pastor of the Boston church, which he understood had separated itself from the Established Church of Old England, he discovered, to his disappointment, that no such separation had taken place. He also found, to his utter dismay, that the Puritan leaders in Boston held to the old-time doctrine that the chief duty of the magistrate is to defend religion and take care that the word of God is purely preached, and to remove and destroy "all false service of God."

Roger Williams' soul revolted against this ancient church-and-state regime's domination of the consciences of men, and took public issue with the union of civil and religious institutions. What chance is there, said he, for freedom of conscience and equality before the law? Later he espoused the cause of the Anabaptists, who declared that the magistrate is not to meddle with religion or matters of conscience, nor compel men to this or that form of religion, because Christ is the King and Lawgiver of the church and conscience.

They did not accept "toleration" of the rights of minority religions on the part of the state church, as a guaranty to religious liberty. "Toleration," they said, "was a mere grant" of religious rights by a superior force which might at any time be withdrawn. Religious liberty is an inherent right and "inalienable," which no earthly power has a right

to abridge. The Anabaptists demanded the absolute freedom of religion from civil control, and
Roger Williams was determined to go to the root
of the matter and secure this absolute freedom in
religious matters for the individual, so that the
liberties of all men might be made secure in civil
government.

The doctrine of absolute freedom in religious
matters for the individual was a despised dogma,
and was destined to bring persecution upon its advo-
cates. There was no congenial soil in Europe for
such a radical doctrine of religious liberty. Those
who advocated it were hunted down like wild ani-
mals and given no quarter. The persecuted looked
to the New World as the only hope of escape, and
as the only place where the seeds of liberty might
take root and yield a benign fruitage. Roger Williams, the noblest of all the reformers in Europe,
who of them all had the clearest view of the proper
relationship of church and state, realized that religious freedom was foredoomed in the Old World
and that the only hope of launching a successful
experiment of a free church in a free state was in
the New World, in virgin territory. In Europe
the legal precedents of centuries, hoary tradition,
the conventional requirements of organized society,
the political and ecclesiastical authorities of whatever name, as well as the teachings in the schools,
were all prejudiced against it and determined to
smother the doctrine of a complete separation of

church and state. Europe would go no farther than to tolerate religious minorities. This doctrine of "toleration" is still the ruling principle of all European governments, and whenever a government goes totalitarian, the state dominates religion and frequently withdraws all protection from religious minorities. Under a totalitarian government neither civil nor religious rights are secure, and religious liberty is a minus quantity.

Roger Williams looked to the New World as the only hope of the promise of better things. He was willing to sacrifice all honors and preferments that might accrue to his advancement along material lines, in order that he might aid in the establishment of absolute religious freedom in the New World. The Puritans had already preceded him with the avowed purpose of enjoying religious freedom for themselves, but not of granting the same privileges to others of divergent faith. They were already persecuting dissenters and nonconformists to their peculiar religious customs and doctrines. Religious prejudices and hatreds over church creeds, and the age-long strife over which should be the dominant and ruling religion or church in the state, were being revived with their ancient fervor. America needed a prophet and a champion of the new conception of religious liberty and of church-and-state separatism. God had prepared a man and sent him to the New World to make it ultimately what He in His wisdom and eternal purpose had designed it to become—an asylum for the oppressed of all nations, "the land of the free and the home of the brave!"

Though an exile, like Moses of old, Roger Williams was sent of God to bring deliverance to God's persecuted and afflicted people in America, which was to them a land of promise as verily as was ancient Palestine to the afflicted children of Israel. Of all the great Protestant reformers, he was the ablest, the best trained, the most enthusiastic, and he held the clearest conceptions of the rights of all men, of religious freedom in religious concerns, and of the true relationship of the church and the state. He was a star of the first magnitude, heralding the coming of a new freedom in a new nation, which was to enlighten the world with a new conception of Christianity and religious freedom.

The new prophet was not well received in New England by the theocratic religionists, and he was soon driven out of Massachusetts by the Puritans for teaching what they denominated as "treasonable and damnable heresy." To teach that the civil magistrate had no right to punish offenses against God and religion was more than the Puritans could tolerate. To cast him out was God's way of bringing him into his own heritage which He had reserved for him. In Rhode Island, which was virgin soil in the wilderness, he founded a commonwealth, a miniature republic, "a government of the people, by the people, and for the people," where, for the first time in history, religious liberty for every man was recognized in civil government as a foundation principle. Roger Williams was the apostle of religious liberty—of soul liberty in the New World. He had the high honor, in the providence of God, of being the first man to establish in practice the emancipation of the conscience of man from the fetters of politico-ecclesiastical rule. He became the harbinger of religious liberty in its true sense and reality, and pointed the true way for the greatest Republic of a free and democratic people. We Americans owe a debt of gratitude to Roger Williams—as preacher, prophet, and statesman—which we cannot pay in any better way than to defend and preserve the precious heritage of civil and religious liberty which he has bequeathed to posterity for the benefit of all mankind.

His ideal of the proper relationship of church and state and his political philosophy and principles of government perhaps cannot be summed up in a more concise form than in his own words:

"The civil sword may make a nation of hypocrites, and anti-Christians, but not one Christian." "Forcing of conscience is a soul-rape." "Persecution for conscience [hath been] the lancet that letteth [the] blood of kings and kingdoms." "Man hath no power to make laws to bind conscience." "The civil commonwealth and the spiritual commonwealth, the church, not inconsistent, though independent, the one on the other." "The civil magistrate owes to false worshipers, (1) permission, (2) protection."

If this fundamental principle of civil government had always been recognized and followed, there never would have been any religious persecution in this world.

Roger Williams not only believed and taught this principle of government, but he practiced it. After having successfully operated this experiment in Rhode Island for twenty-seven years, he embodied, in 1663, in the memorial charter for the Commonwealth and English Colony of Rhode Island his fundamental tenet, as follows:

"No person within the said colony, at any time hereafter, shall be in any wise molested, punished, disquieted, or called in question, for any differences in opinion, in matters of religion, who do not actually disturb the civil peace of our said colony; but that all and every person and persons may, from time to time, and at all times hereafter, freely and fully have and enjoy his own and their own judgments and consciences, in matters of religious concernments, throughout the tract of land hereafter mentioned, they behaving themselves peaceably and quietly and not using this liberty to licentiousness and profaneness, nor to the civil injury or outward disturbance of others."

In this charter are set forth the matchless provisions which were incorporated one hundred and twenty-six years later in the Federal Constitution of the United States of America, "Congress shall make no law respecting an establishment of religion, or prohibiting the free exercise thereof," and similar provisions in the respective State constitutions.

Thus Roger Williams became the builder of the ideals of a new nation, which was destined to influence the ideals of many other nations. The equality of all men and of all religions before the law, without special privileges and preferences to any, was the cardinal principle in the government founded by Roger Williams. He not only legislated for his day, but, as he hoped, for "all times hereafter." As long as men conducted themselves "peaceably" and "civilly," they were not to be punished on account of their religious beliefs or practices. No one was to suffer any civil disability by reason of his religious favor, provided he respected the equal rights of all others.

Especially was Roger Williams opposed to any financial alliances between the church and the state such as compelled people to be taxed by the state for the aid and support of any sort of religion. He did not believe that any person elected to public office should ever take advantage of his public office through legislation or the administration of his civil duties, to promote the religious interests of religious organizations, nor should he ever attempt to settle religious controversies by law, or give preference by judicial decisions to religious

Statue of Roger Williams in Capitol

Congress, in 1864, invited each State in the Union to send statues of two of its most illustrious citizens for permanent preservation in the hall of fame in the Capitol. Many have responded, among them the State of Rhode Island. Naturally enough, Rhode Island is represented in the National Statuary Hall by a marble figure of Roger Williams. It is the work of Franklin Simmonds. In his left hand is a book upon which are the words, "Soul Liberty, 1636." The life, work, and ideals of Roger Williams as portrayed in this book reveal that he had more to do with shaping the foundation principles of the American Republic than any other man. The founders of the American Republic were inspired by his writings and ideals, and sought to incorporate them into the Bill of Rights in the Constitution.

opinions, creeds, usages, or customs. His attachment to the equality of all men before the law, placed a self-restraint upon the exercise of his own liberty concerning his own religious creed while exercising the functions of public office.

Roger Williams lived in advance of his age. The New World was not yet ready to adopt his liberal ideals. While he held strong religious convictions, he did not allow those convictions to develop in him the spirit of intolerance toward his opponents. The most difficult lesson which mankind must learn and keep constantly in mind, especially when one is entrusted with power and authority over others, is that religious truth, which we deem most precious and paramount, can never be advanced through coercion upon others. The purest faith can become corrupt by the employment of unholy and unsanctified means and measures to promote it. In fact, the adherents of the purest and most exalted faith are ever tempted to employ the instrument of misguided zeal in the hope of its advancement.

Roger Williams lived in the days when bigotry and intolerance were making war against all who attempted to follow their own religious convictions independently of the established state religion. Whatever religion happened to be the state religion, whether Protestant or Catholic, the individual who had religious opinions of his own was not allowed to practice them. He was haunted and hunted night and day, and denied all semblance of liberty—both civil and religious. It cost something to be an independent and free Christian in those days of religious intolerance and persecution.

Roger Williams denied the right of the civil government to rule in all things, both temporal and spiritual. All governments in Europe were either totalitarian or authoritarian in form or in practice. No man could call his soul his own. He existed solely for the benefit of the state. All his activities in life were regulated, regimented, and restricted. Some of the governments in Europe today are reverting to the medieval type, and the results are conditions similar to those of medieval times. Whenever the consciences of men are controlled by the civil authorities, the destruction of liberty— both civil and religious—always follows. Wherever religious dogma is made subservient to the authority of the state, those who dissent from the state religion are regarded as enemies of both religion and the state.

Those who attempt by legislative authority and arbitrary power to dominate the consciences of all men in all things, both temporal and spiritual, do so under the mistaken conception that they are keeping the true religion from being perverted and corrupted; but as a matter of fact, these self-appointed protectors of religion become, through their ill-conceived and misguided zeal and devotion, the real perverters and corrupters of religion.

Roger Williams struggled manfully to put an end to religious intolerance and persecution. By advocating the principle of essential justice and the equality of all men before the law, irrespective of religious creed, nationality, or race, he struck a death blow to the totalitarian and authoritarian forms of government. His seeds of truth and liberty and justice for all men alike, found deep root in American soil, and it was in America that he finally succeeded in establishing his ideal form of government—that after which the American Republic was modeled more than a century later. We must look to Roger Williams, more than to Jefferson or Madison, as the true builder of our American Bill of Rights, because all the provisions of civil and religious liberty as set forth in the matchless Constitution of the United States, were incorporated in principle in the charter of Rhode Island as conceived and framed by Roger Williams.

Both Jefferson and Madison had the writings of this first and greatest of all Americans who formed the ideals and principles of civil government in Rhode Island, and they gave vital breath to those immortal and immutable principles of human rights and liberties in the Declaration of Independence and in the Bill of Rights of the Federal Constitution of the American Republic. The great apostle of soul liberty was the instrument that gave inspiration and guidance to the shaping of the fundamental law of a nation which was

3

that interposed a barrier betwixt men and the fellowship of their dreams."

Roger Williams was a rebel from his youth against everything that fettered the conscience. In writing of his childhood experiences to Governor Winthrop after his early conversion to the tenets of the Puritan faith, he says, "Myself but a child in everything, though in Christ called and persecuted even in and out of my father's house these twenty years."

He dared to oppose his parents in religious matters. They stood high in the political, social, and religious order of that day, and to rebel in religious matters against the authority of a parent or of the state church, was no light matter in those times. A nonconformist, or Puritan, under James I, was severely persecuted. Many of the Puritan sect were burned at the stake in Smithfield at the time when young Williams was converted to that faith. His parents lived just a few doors beyond Newgate Prison, or the Smithfield plaza, where the so-called heretics were burned, and the parents' anxiety for young Roger led them to employ strenuous methods to change his mind back to the state religion, but it was of no avail. All their parental entreaties and harsh methods failed to turn "the erring child from his dissenting ways." When they entreated him to "believe as the church believes," the young Puritan, newly converted, replied: "The truth is, . . . the Father of light and mercies hath touched my soul with a love to Himself, to His only-begotten and true Lord Jesus, and to His Holy Scriptures." Such an argument was unanswerable, and that was the kind of argument which characterized all of Roger Williams' answers to his adversaries.

All through his life he met opposition, for he was in advance of the times. He wrote to Mr. John Whipple, Jr., in 1669: "I have been used to bear censures and reproaches for truth's sake, for reproving and witnessing against the works of darkness above these fifty years." But the censure, the reproach, and the threats of parents, of friends, of the authorities of the state church, could not dampen the courage or break the spirit of young Roger Williams. In his old age he was as fearless and daring as he had been in his youth for the cause of truth and religious liberty.

The year prior to his conversion to the Puritan faith, a certain prominent legate had been burned at the stake at Smithfield, and evidently this event made a deep impression on young Roger's mind, and led him to investigate the Puritan faith more fully, which resulted in his conversion.

On his mother's side, Roger Williams was connected with the prominent Pemberton family, which rose to great political influence in England after the Reformation. These family connections brought him into a prominent social and political environment among the gentility at the opening of the seventeenth century. It was these connections

Williams Stenographer to Lord Coke

Young Williams was stenographer to the Star Chamber, a noted London court. There he met his mentor, the distinguished English jurist, Sir Edward Coke, whom he dearly loved and greatly respected. Lord Coke encouraged the lad to study law and obtain the highest possible general education obtainable in the universities of London. After pursuing the study of law and the science of government, he abandoned it and turned to theology, in the hope he might labor for the Lord of the universe rather than the rulers of England, who exercised such arbitrary authority in religious matters. Young Williams imbibed the spirit of independent thinking from Lord Coke and learned much in statescraft that was very profitable to him when he finally founded a civil state of his own in Rhode Island.

38

which gained him special political favors and advantages later in life, relative to the establishment of his republic in the New World as an independent territory for his new experiment in government.

Roger Williams grew up in a stimulating intellectual environment, with many colorful contrasts. During his boyhood and early manhood, Shakespeare finished his greatest works and died. Lord Bacon revised his essays, from which Williams quoted profusely in his defense of religious-liberty principles. He was a student under Sir Edward Coke, the eminent English jurist who defied the royal authority and wrote the "Institutes," now a classic in common law and a defense of the rights of the people. In his early teens he joined the religious protest of the Puritans against the established church-and-state order, and he chose the political faith of John Eliot and Sir Edward Coke.

Because of Roger's skill in shorthand and his training in legal procedure in the courts of England, Sir Edward Coke chose him as his secretary to take notes of the proceedings in the Star Chamber and to take down his legal opinions and speeches. Young Williams must have been an expert stenographer, for Mrs. Anne Sadlier, daughter of Sir Edward Coke, recorded on the back of a letter from Williams in 1652: "This Roger Williams, when he was a youth, would, in shorthand, take sermons and speeches in the Star Chamber and present them to my dear father. He, seeing so hopeful a youth, took such a liking to him that he sent him to Sutton's Hospital (Charter House), and he was the second that was placed there; full little did he think that he would have proved such a rebel to God, the king, and his country."

But Sir Edward Coke, chief justice of the King's Bench, the foremost authority in English law at that time, dared in points of law to withstand Queen Elizabeth and King James when he defended the sovereignty of Parliament and the rights of the people under the common law against the claims of the sovereigns of England. While taking down the speeches of Chief Justice Coke, Williams acquired a fuller understanding of the principles of law and government and the rights of the people and of Parliament, which he applied practically in the building of his model republic in the New World.

That he imbibed many of his liberal ideals from Coke, Roger Williams fully acknowledged when he wrote to Mrs. Anne Sadlier in 1652, and paid the highest respect to those sterling qualities which he admired in her father, saying:

"My much-honored friend, that man of honor and wisdom and piety, your dear father, was often pleased to call me his son; and truly it was as bitter as death . . . to me, when I rode past Windsor Way to take ship at Bristow and saw Stoke House where the blessed man was. . . . But how many thousand times since have I had honorable and precious remembrance of his person and the life, the writings, the speeches, and the examples of that glorious light. And I may truly say that besides my natural inclination to study and activity, his example, instruction, and encouragement have spurred me on to a more than ordinary industrious and patient course in my whole course hitherto. .... What I have done and suffered,—and I hope for the truth of God, . . . you may acknowledge some beams of His holy wisdom and goodness, who hath not suffered all your own and your dear father's smiles to have been lost upon so poor and despicable an object. .... I hope for God, that, as your honorable father was wont to say, he that shall harrow what I have sown must rise early."

The "much-honored friend," Lord Coke, nominated Roger Williams for a scholarship to the Charter House in 1621, when he was eighteen years old. Later on, he won an appointment to Cambridge University. In the chapel cloister of the Charter House is a memorial to Roger Williams, and in the Hall of Fame in the Capitol building, Washington, D.C., is a marble statue of Roger Williams holding in his hands a Bible upon which is carved: "The Apostle of Soul Liberty." In Geneva, Switzerland, in the midst of the statues of the great Reformers of the Reformation and the Renaissance, stands in bold relief the statue of Roger Williams as the great reformer, leading all reformers of the reformation in America.

Entering Charter House School

Sir Edward Coke not only recognized young Williams' skill in shorthand when he served as his secretary, but his aptitude in the science of government. Later he placed him as a student in Charter House School. After finishing this school, Williams attended Pembroke College in Cambridge. He was serious and studious, and improved every opportunity to gain knowledge that would enable him to be of service in uplifting humanity and society to a higher level. Being religiously inclined, he early accepted the established state religion of England. However, he was unable to reconcile its practices with the teachings of Christ. He took issue with Archbishop Laud, who imposed great hardships upon all dissenters. This brought the wrath of Archbishop Laud down upon his head, and made his flight to America necessary.

42

At Cambridge University, in 1623, when he was twenty years of age, Roger Williams took up the religious and social protests of the Puritans and reformers and under the able leadership of Lord Edward Coke, who was High Steward of Cambridge University, and of Sir John Eliot, joined the party opposing Bishop Laud's church policy and the followers of the king.   In 1627 Williams received his degree of A.B. from Cambridge, after which he began his studies more specifically for the ministry.   His religious studies turned him against the state church, and he left Cambridge in 1629, after taking two years of postgraduate work, discontented with the political and religious atmosphere of the university under the dominating zeal of Bishop William Laud.

Sir Edward Coke and other prominent friends endeavored to secure him a position which would afford him a good living.   But a "tender conscience," said Williams, "kept me from honor and preferment.   Besides many former offers and that late New England call, I have since had two several livings proffered to me."   The officials of the Massachusetts Bay Colony proffered him the call from New England to become pastor of the Salem church.

Drastic steps were taken in 1630 by King Charles and Bishop Laud to stem the tide of liberalism and to blot out Puritanism and other dissenting sectarianism against the established church.   The king resorted to physical torture and disfigurement, fines, imprisonment, and whippings of all ardent dissenters. King James had already sent Lord Edward Coke with Pym and Selden to the London Tower, for writing and supporting the protestation against political Catholicism, Arminianism, and the divine right of the king. Many persons fled to Holland for safety, but Roger Williams and other leading Puritans fled to the American wilderness.

Mr. Williams had written his "Dissent" against Bishop Laud's formal service of the Book of Common Prayer, and the bishop was seeking his apprehension and pursued him out of the land. He decided to accept the late New England call. His arrival in Boston on February 5, 1631, marked the beginning of a famous episode in American history.

A FABLE FOR CRITICS

And I honor the man who is willing to sink
Half his present repute for the freedom to think,
And when he has thought, be his cause strong or weak,
Will risk t'other half for the freedom to speak,
Caring nought for what vengeance the mob has in store,
Let the mob be the upper ten thousand or lower.

—*James Russell Lowell.*

Arrival and Open Break With Church and State Authorities

We have briefly covered, thus far, the life and work of Roger Williams until he was compelled to flee to America for safety from religious persecutors in Europe. But the paramount reason for his coming to America was to preach the gospel in all its fullness, and to help create a republic in the New World in which the natural rights of all men would be respected before the law, and in which the conscience of the individual would be supreme in the religious realm without civil molestation.

Roger Williams was compelled to flee from England under persecutions by Bishop Laud, or surrender his religious convictions; "and for him, as for all noblest natures," says Judge Durfee, in speaking of his flight, "a life of transparent truthfulness was alone an instinct and a necessity. This

Williams' Arrival in America

Roger Williams and his wife, Mary, arrived in America at what is now the Boston harbor, early in 1631. The Puritans had preceded him by one year and had a good-sized settlement established at Boston and another at Salem, but the Pilgrim Fathers had preceded the Puritans by ten years. The Puritans were established as the Massachusetts Bay Colony and the Pilgrims as the Plymouth Colony at Plymouth. Hailed as a "godly minister," and one whom the common people heard gladly, he was invited to speak in the Boston church upon his arrival. But he had been called to the pastorate of the Salem church. The officials of the Boston church-and-state discovered that he was an independent thinker. He soon entered upon his pastoral duties at Salem with sincerity and devotion.

absolute sincerity is the key to his character, as it was always the mainspring of his conduct. It was this which led him to reject indignantly the compromises with his conscience which from time to time were proposed to him. It was this which impelled him when he discovered a truth to proclaim it, when he detected an error to expose it, when he saw an evil to try and remedy it, and when he could do a good, even to his enemies, to do it."

Upon his arrival in Boston on February 5, 1631, Roger Williams was welcomed with open arms, and the ecclesiastical authorities invited him to succeed Mr. Wilson, who was about to return to England, as a teacher in the Boston church. The Boston Puritans believed their church to be the "most glorious on earth," and they were astonished because Roger Williams felt conscientiously bound to decline their invitation because that church was still "unseparated" from the Established Church of England and was under Bishop Laud's control.

Roger Williams, possessing the religious convictions which he cherished, had good reasons for refusing a pastorate in any church that was still officially connected with the Established Church of England. In his home district in England, from which he fled, he had just witnessed, before he sailed to America, the persecution in all its hellish cruelty, of Doctor Leighton, who had become a Puritan. Neal, in his "History of the Puritans," tells of Doctor Leighton's arrest and of the in-

tion that the civil magistrates had "no rights as such, to rule in spiritual matters," struck the New England Puritans with wonder and amazement, as the whole system of the "Holy Commonwealth" of the Bay Colony was based upon the Bible as their statute book; and the ten commandments as a whole, as they interpreted them, were the warp and woof of their whole social fabric as administered by the clergy and the magistrates. The Puritans believed, as many religious legalists believe today, that if the violations of the first four commandments of the decalogue, which are purely offenses against God, are not punished by the civil magistrate, religion will be destroyed and civil society cannot exist. But Roger Williams believed that religion would flourish and the state would prosper when they are entirely separated from each other.

By refusing the best "call" in New England, and asking the Boston church to separate itself from the state religion, Roger Williams created a dilemma for the Boston Puritans. They violently disagreed with him, and would have ordered him sent back to England, but they did not dare for fear of losing the friendship and support of Sir William Masham, a member of the company in England, Sir Thomas Barrington, Earl of Warwick, Sir Oliver St. Johns, Sir Henry Martin, and many other influential friends of Williams in England.

In the meanwhile, Williams received a "call" from the Salem church to serve as its pastor, to the

Witnessed Doctor Leighton's Persecution

Just before he fled from England, Roger Williams had witnessed the inhuman treatment accorded Doctor Leighton under Archbishop Laud's ecclesiastical sentence. The doctor was fined, brought to the pillory and publicly whipped, had his ears cut off, his nose split, his face branded, and was shut up in prison for the rest of his life. The Puritans had fled to America to escape this religio-political persecution, but strange to say, they exhibited the same intolerant spirit against Roger Williams and others who held divergent views. The Puritans in America employed the whipping post, confiscation of property, and banishment "to open the understanding of the heretics," in order, as they said, to save them from hell-fire. Such is the inevitable result of a state-enforced religion.

great alarm of the magistrates and elders at Boston. The court at Boston held a special session to consider the matter, and it decided to write a letter of warning to the Salem church and to Mr. Endicott to this effect, that whereas Mr. Williams taught that the Boston church should separate itself from the legal Established Church of England, and besides had declared his opinion that "the magistrate might not punish the breach of the Sabbath nor any other offense that was a breach of the first table," therefore the court marveled that Salem would choose him without advising with the council, and withal desired that they would forbear to proceed till they had conferred about it.

The Salem church, jealous of its independent rights, gave the magistrates and clergy of Boston the rebuke they so richly deserved, and insisted that Roger Williams accept their call and enter upon his charge at once, which he did. Here Williams preached his views freely, and the freemen of Salem welcomed him with open arms. But the spiritual dictators and autocrats of Boston hounded his steps and stirred up an active opposition against him in the colony outside the town of Salem. The cruel hand of persecution was lifted against him, and inside of six months he was forced to retire to Plymouth and seek refuge among the Pilgrims, who held far more liberal views toward dissenters than did the Puritans.

For the next two years, Roger Williams

preached at Plymouth as assistant pastor to Elder
Smith, and the independent colony of Plymouth
protected him from persecution by Massachusetts
Bay. His teachings were well received by the people of Plymouth, and Governor Bradford esteemed
him highly. While here he did missionary work
among the Indian tribes, and entered into a treaty
agreement with Massasoit and other Indian chiefs,
which laid the foundation for the establishment of
Rhode Island a little later, when he was banished
the second time from Salem. It was well for him
that he stayed two years at Plymouth and won his
way into their hearts, for his Plymouth friends
served as a buffer ally between the Bay Colony
and the Providence Plantation.

The Pilgrims also had a union of church and
state, and punished and persecuted those who broke
the first four commandments of the decalogue, but
they were more mild and tolerant than the Puritans.
Roger Williams became restless under the Plymouth theocracy, and hoped they would improve
affairs. In the summer of 1633 he received a second "call" to assume the pastorate of the Salem
church, which he gladly accepted.

The return to Salem marked the beginning of
a series of controversies between the authorities of
Salem and Boston. The Puritan clergy of Boston
were so strongly Calvinistic that their new-founded
utopia, which they styled the "Holy Commonwealth," gave no quarter to religious dissenters

They believed that it was their duty to see that all men "obeyed the inexorable will of God," not as each individual understood it, but as the Puritan theocracy interpreted it. This theory led to the justification of the most cruel persecutions ever perpetrated upon dissenters, except, perhaps, for the atrocities of the Inquisition.

All this persecution was done in the name of God and for the good of the church and the state. The civil magistrate and the civil law were used as the vehicle to carry forward the dogmas and propaganda of the Puritan church. Theocracy and oligarchy combined to share the spoils of religious and civil power. The most powerful weapons they employed were the whipping post, confiscation of property, and banishment. They held that they were justified "to use the sword of the civil magistrate to open the understanding of the heretics," in order to save them from hell-fire.

Roger Williams charged that the New England clergy, "under a pretense of holy orders in themselves, put over the drudgery of execution to their enslaved seculars." "I affirm there was never civil state in the world," declared Williams, "that ever did or ever shall make good work of it, with a civil sword in spiritual matters." Instead, the state should give "free and absolute permission of conscience to all men in what is merely spiritual."

Years later Cotton Mather remarked in his "Magnalia," "There was a whole country in Amer-

ica like to be set on fire by the rapid motion of a
windmill in the head of one particular man." That
man was Roger Williams, whose opinions relative
to the limitation of civil magistrates in the exercise
of their proper functions, excluding their authority
in spiritual matters, had within two and a half years
set all New England on fire, and what hurt most
was that the common people heard him gladly.

In April, 1634, the magistrates ordered all Bay
residents who were not freemen to take a Resident's
Oath, pledging themselves to submit to the orders
of the General Court. On May 14, 1634, the court
passed a new Freeman's Oath, which required the
freemen to pledge allegiance to the General Court
and officers. The purpose was to eradicate all opposition to the "Holy Commonwealth," and the
penalty for refusing to take the oath was banishment.

The new oath was evidently aimed at Roger
Williams, as it sanctioned "the right of magistrates
to punish for breaches of the first table and to rule
in religion." Williams accepted the challenge, and
denied the right of the state to enforce an oath
which was in fact "a spiritual form and act of
worship and prayer," and he attacked its legality
so vehemently that he swayed public opinion
against it, and made it impossible for the court to
enforce the oath. He became the people's champion in the cause of liberty, and his victory made
him very popular in Salem. The religio-political

authorities of the "Holy Commonwealth" found metal of no common temper in Roger Williams.

Some new occasion must be found to apprehend this "first rebel against the divine church order established in the wilderness." They determined to subdue Williams or banish him. Through guile and threats, the General Court finally won John Endicott, Mr. Williams' defender and friend, over to its side. By the same means, the court officials succeeded in turning the majority of the Salem church against him. Finally Roger Williams was summoned for trial on the charge of entertaining "dangerous opinions." The Bay governor, twenty-five court magistrates, the deputies, and all the ministers of the Bay were present. It was the most spectacular assembly and trial, and the most far-reaching in its results, that ever convened in America, aside from the Continental Congress of 1776, which was made possible only by the courageous stand of Roger Williams at this eventful trial.

The clergy as the advisers to the General Court gave an inquisitorial color to the whole procedure. They acted in conjunction with the court, at once as legislators, executives, and judiciary—judge, jury, and final court of appeal—in the trial of Roger Williams, against whom they were also the complaining witnesses. There was, for Roger Williams, no more hope of escape from this inquisition than there would have been if he had been held in the jaws of a crocodile.

Williams' Defense Before General Court

Williams, championing the cause of liberty, won many friends. The General Court of Massachusetts Bay Colony decided that he must be subdued or banished. So, through guile and threats, this high authority won to its side John Endicott and a majority of the Salem church. Finally Roger Williams was summoned to trial on the charge of entertaining "dangerous opinions." Before the Bay governor, twenty-five court magistrates, the deputies, and all the Puritan ministers of the Bay, he eloquently argued in defense of his principles, and, like Luther, he stood unshaken in the "rockie strength" of his convictions. He was sentenced by the governor to banishment from the colony. That sentence was the harbinger of religious liberty in America.

Governor Haynes, presiding officer of the court, was chief prosecuting attorney and the judge who was to pronounce the sentence. Roger Williams had no attorney to defend his case, as none, through fear, dared to defend him. Undaunted and alone, like Christ, he faced the inquisitorial court and stood in the "rockie strength" of his principles. He pleaded his case so eloquently and logically that he forced a division between the magistrates and deputies. Not for nought had he sat at the feet of Sir Edward Coke in the Star Chamber of England. With the courage of a Luther, he launched his broadsides against fifty of the ablest men of Massachusetts Bay Colony.

The ministers moved among the magistrates and deputies who were favorable to Mr. Williams to turn their votes against him. The lobbying was successful, and the "holy brethren" rejoiced in securing his conviction.

Before sentence of banishment was pronounced, the court gave him a chance to recant. Would he recant, or would he stand his ground like Luther? Upon his decision depended the future of Rhode Island, yea, more—to a large extent the future of America and of the world. Worn out and desperate, through lengthy hours of disputation, would he lose heart and yield? Never! never! He stood unshaken as the eternal hills in the "rockie strength" of his convictions. "I shall be ready . . . not only to be bound and banished, but to die also in New

England" for the truth, declared Williams. So
hour after hour he argued in defense of his principles, unsubdued and undismayed, till the sun
sank into darkness and the weary court adjourned,
hoping that he might recant on the morrow. In
this hope they were disappointed.

The next morning, October 9, 1635, Roger Williams made it known that he was as unshaken as
the Rock of Gibraltar, and that he had faith to
believe that the principles he advocated would
triumph, even if he were killed.

One of the laws enacted by the Massachusetts
Bay Colony was: "If any person or persons within
this jurisdiction . . . shall deny their [the magistrates'] lawful right or authority . . . to punish the
outward breaches of the first table [of the deca-
logue], . . . every such person or persons shall be
sentenced to banishment." As Roger Williams
stoutly denied the jurisdiction of the civil magistrates in religious matters covered by the first four
commandments written upon the first table of the
decalogue, he was condemned to banishment.

It was well understood by the Puritans that the
first table of the decalogue embraced the first four
commandments, and the second table, the last six
commandments. Roger Williams pointed out that
the first four commandments of the law of God
enjoined purely spiritual and religious duties which
the individual owed to God, and that the violation
of these four commandments—namely, the refusal

to recognize Jehovah as the one and only supreme God, the worshiping of images, taking God's name in vain, and refusing to observe the Sabbath as a day of worship and rest—was an offense against God and religion which the civil magistrate had no right in justice to punish. He held that whenever a human being attempted to judge another individual in matters of conscience and religion, the judge was assuming the prerogatives of God and would have to sit as a discerner of the motives of a man's heart, which required divine discernment.

The first four commandments of the decalogue prescribe a man's duties toward God, and the last six, a man's duties toward his fellow man. Therefore, Roger Williams contended, the civil magistrate, who rightfully could deal only with civil matters, had no authority in justice to enforce the commandments upon the first table of the decalogue. If the civil magistrates and legislators had always recognized this line of distinction between the first and the second table of the decalogue, there never would have been formed a union between the church and the state, and religious persecution would have been impossible. The failure to recognize a line of demarcation between the duties we owe to Caesar and the obligations we owe to God has been the root cause of all religious persecutions, as well as of bitter experiences which have come to religion. Politics and religion never did form a friendly mixture, and the sooner the state and the church learn this lesson, the better it will be for both. Roger Williams finally demonstrated this truth in his experiment in Rhode Island by completely separating the church and the state and permitting the civil magistrate to function "only in civil things."

He was accused of advancing opinions that were dangerous to the peace and order of the commonwealth; but in Rhode Island he founded a community in which perfect religious liberty prevailed, and in which his doctrines and teachings were given free course; yet life, property, peace, and order were far more secure than they were in Puritan Massachusetts, where life, property, and peace were frequently sacrificed for conscience' sake. He demonstrated beyond question that his teachings promoted peace and order in the state, and that the charges against him were unsustained and his banishment was unjustifiable. It was thus that a kind Providence permitted the evil which befell him in Salem, Massachusetts, to enable him to work out a system of government in Rhode Island which not only constituted a requital for the injustice he had suffered, but served as a model for the great American Republic.

That sentence of exile, instead of being the doom of religious liberty in America, was its harbinger. It opened the door of opportunity to establish a model republic as an asylum for the oppressed of America and of Europe, where all could worship God unmolested, in harmony with the dictates of their own consciences. It enabled Roger Williams to do for America and for the world what would have been impossible within the Holy Commonwealth.

The Honorable Oscar S. Straus, twice American ambassador to Turkey, and Secretary of Labor and Commerce in the Cabinet of the late President Theodore Roosevelt, fittingly spoke thus of Roger Williams: "If I were asked to select from all the great men who have left their impress upon this continent; . . . if I were asked whom to hold before the American people and the world to typify the American spirit of fairness, of freedom, of liberty in church and state, I would without any hesitation select that great prophet who established the first political community on the basis of a free church in a free state, the great and immortal Roger Williams."

STANZAS ON FREEDOM

Men! whose boast it is that ye
Come of fathers brave and free,
If there breathe on earth a slave,
Are ye truly free and brave?
If ye do not feel the chain,
When it works a brother's pain,
Are ye not base slaves indeed,
Slaves unworthy to be freed?

Women! who shall one day bear
Sons to breathe New England air,
If ye hear, without a blush,
Deeds to make the roused blood rush
Like red lava through your veins,
For your sisters now in chains—
Answer! are ye fit to be
Mothers of the brave and free?

Is true freedom but to break
Fetters for our own dear sake,
And, with leathern hearts, forget
That we owe mankind a debt?
No! true freedom is to share
All the chains our brothers wear,
And, with heart and hand, to be
Earnest to make others free!

They are slaves who fear to speak
For the fallen and the weak;
They are slaves who will not choose
Hatred, scoffing, and abuse,
Rather than in silence shrink
From the truth they needs must think:
They are slaves who dare not be
In the right with two or three.

—*James Russell Lowell.*

His Banishment, Flight, and Subsequent Founding of Rhode Island

After the General Court of Massachusetts Bay Colony had sentenced Roger Williams to banishment, the court granted him six weeks' grace before the sentence was to become effective. The inquisitorial court, in pronouncing sentence of banishment, charged:

"Mr. Roger Williams . . . hath broached and divulged divers new and dangerous opinions against the authority of magistrates . . . and churches, . . . and yet maintaineth the same without retraction: it is therefore ordered that the same Mr. Williams shall depart out of this jurisdiction within six weeks next ensuing, . . . not to return any more without license from the court."

Cotton Mather, a prominent Puritan clergyman of Massachusetts, denounced Williams as the "first rebel against the divine church order estab-

63

Bids Good-by to Wife and Babe

The court ordered the banishment of Roger Williams from the Massachusetts Bay Colony to be enforced within six weeks. He was stigmatized the "first rebel against the divine church order established in the wilderness," by Cotton Mather, a Puritan clergyman. His defense in behalf of religious freedom had awakened public sympathy and made him popular among the common people. Henry Vane, Jr., from England, and others, visited him; but this friendly intercourse only enraged the authorities, and his immediate arrest was ordered. They planned to take him by surprise and exile him to England. A secret friend, however, sent him a timely warning. Williams sensed his danger, and heeding the warning, bade his wife and babe a fond farewell, and escaped into the friendly wilderness.

lished in the wilderness." But the gallant defense which Roger Williams made before the court in behalf of the rights of the people and of the fundamental principles of religious freedom under a complete separation of church and state, awakened public sympathy in his behalf, and made him more popular than ever among the common people. His popularity excited the envy and jealousy of the theocratic court leaders.

What added fuel to the fire was the arrival in New England, two days after the famous trial, of Henry Vane, Jr., the twenty-three-year-old son of Sir Henry Vane. This liberal and cultured gentleman, who afterward became one of England's illustrious statesmen, immediately sought the companionship of Roger Williams, and was captivated by the gracious charm and noble sentiments of this champion of religious liberty, who was ten years his senior. They began an association of friendship and mutual helpfulness which meant much to the development of the little republic Williams was about to establish. Other people visited the home of Roger Williams, and he, being of a friendly and hospitable spirit, welcomed all his guests and talked with them. This exercise of freedom of speech the General Court declared was unlawful. Accordingly, Governor Haynes and his court assistants, on January 11, 1636, decided to act immediately, before the time set for Williams' banishment matured. They ordered

5

Captain Underhill, with fourteen men, to take Roger Williams by surprise in the night, and place him on board a waiting ship to be sent into exile in England, where he could give them no more trouble. Governor Winthrop, who was his secret friend, sent a timely warning to Williams, and before the heretic hunters reached Salem, Mr. Williams, at the hour of midnight, bade his wife and newborn babe a loving farewell, and through a blinding snow, facing a frigid blast, fled into the wilderness. What he had to endure and suffer as he was driven, unexpectedly, from his home, in midwinter, by his persecutors, is best described in the few fragmentary references he made later to this perilous journey to the camp of friendly Indians along the Narragansett Bay. Briefly, Williams wrote:

"I was unmercifully driven from my chamber to a winter's flight, exposed to the miseries, poverties, necessities, wants, debts, hardships of sea and land in a banished condition. . . . I was sorely tossed for one fourteen weeks in a bitter winter season, not knowing what bread and bed did mean."

Not only did he wander through the deep snow of the wilderness without bread or bed, but without bow or arrow, spear or club, hatchet or gun, where no white man had ever trod, eating roots, nuts, and acorns as he searched for them under the deep snows, until he finally reached the wigwams along the Narragansett Bay, where he found shelter among the red-skinned barbarians. Be it said to the everlasting shame of his Christian persecutors that the savage Indians of North America became the conservators of American liberty, instead of the white man.

Roger Williams' great love and kindness for all men conquered the wild, savage element in the bosoms of the untutored Indians, and awakened their sympathies for his sufferings at the hands of his own race. Massasoit and Canonicus, two Narraganset chiefs, took him to their own cabins and showed him the same hospitality they would have shown a brother.

Shortly after his arrival in the camp of Canonicus, trouble broke out between the two rival chiefs, and Canonicus was about to make war upon Massasoit. But Roger Williams, who had gained the confidence and friendship of both these Indian chiefs, traveled back and forth between the tribes, earnestly seeking an agreement of peace between them. He succeeded so well as a peacemaker that Massasoit in gratitude gave him a grant of land for a settlement on the east bank of the Seekonk River.

Roger Williams, in writing of this first venture, says:

"I first pitched and began to build and plant at Seekonk, . . . but I received a letter from my ancient friend Mr. Winslow, then governor of Plymouth,

Williams Fleeing Through Wilderness

Fleeing from home at night, and in the dead of winter, Roger Williams suffered many hardships. He wrote: "I was sorely tossed for one fourteen weeks in a bitter winter season, not knowing what bread and bed did mean." Finally he reached the wigwams along the Narragansett Bay, where he found shelter among the Indians. In gratitude for his having acted as peacemaker between two rival chiefs, Canonicus and Massasoit, the latter gave Williams a grant of land. He started to build and plant, but was warned by the Plymouth Colony that he was within the bounds of the colonies already established, and so he bought land from the Indians on the other side of the Mooshassuc River and named the place Providence. He invited the oppressed of New England and Europe to settle in his new colony.

68

. . . advising me since I was fallen into the edge of their bounds and they were loath to displease the Bay, to remove but to the other side of the water and then, he said, I had the country free before me and might be as free as themselves and we should be loving neighbors together."

By this time some of his persecuted friends in Salem had joined him, and again he pulled up stakes and set out, with a handful of men of kindred spirit, and landed at a spot on the Mooshassuc River, now known as Providence, Rhode Island. He established his permanent home here, and founded, not a colony, but in reality a republic which was to demonstrate that civil government under a complete separation of church and state, granting freedom of conscience in religious matters to each individual, would prosper more than under a church-and-state union. He also sought to establish a popular democratic form of government as the surest basis for the security of human rights.

Roger Williams states that his first and chief concern was to make this new settlement "a shelter to persons distressed for conscience," and to establish "a civil government" which exercised authority "only in civil things." He avowed that "the sovereign power of all civil authority is founded in the consent of the people," and that the majority had no control over the conscience of the individual in religious matters, or over "inalienable rights."

As Bancroft, the great American historian, says:
"He was the first person in modern Christendom
to assert in its plenitude the doctrine of the liberty
of conscience,—the equality of opinions before the
law. . . . Williams would permit persecution of no
opinion, of no religion, leaving heresy unharmed
by law, and orthodoxy unprotected by the terrors
of penal statutes."—*"History of the United States,"
Vol. I, p. 282.*

The persecuted, not only of America, but of
Europe, found perfect freedom in this utopia of
republics. The dissenters of the Massachusetts
Bay Colony were at first banished to Rhode Island.
But later on they fled of their own accord, and
Roger Williams received them all with open arms.
In a short time four separate settlements were es-
tablished in Rhode Island, which were formed
into a confederation, or, rather, a republic, with
Roger Williams as its elected president.

The Puritan colonies of New England formed
a confederation from which they excluded Rhode
Island, or the Providence Plantations. The Puritans assumed a hostile attitude toward Rhode Island,
and Roger Williams was sent to England in 1643
to seek from the English Parliament a charter for
their newly founded republic, and protection
against the aggressive and intolerant Puritans of
the Massachusetts confederation. With the assistance of Sir Henry Vane, a charter was obtained
in 1644, wherein the most complete liberty in the

matter of religion was assured to all the settlers in Rhode Island, and to all those who might unite with them in the future.

In May, 1647, the General Assembly of Rhode Island adopted a code of laws which closed with the declaration, "All men may walk as their consciences persuade them, without molestation—every one in the name of his God." Thus Rhode Island became the first province in America which officially proclaimed full and complete religious liberty to "all men" of every persuasion and of no persuasion. It was not an "act of toleration," which granted a permission to a particular group of professed Christians, as was granted in Maryland in 1649, but a proclamation of religious liberty by natural right to believers and nonbelievers alike.

How sweeping and all-inclusive was the proclamation of universal freedom—"all men." No one was excluded from the provision of religious freedom in Rhode Island. In Maryland religious freedom was granted only to those "professing to believe in Jesus Christ" and to those who believe "God's holy and true Christian religion," and the Maryland Act of Toleration of 1649 expressly provided that "whatsoever person shall blaspheme God, or shall deny or reproach the Holy Trinity, or any of the three Persons thereof, shall be punished with death," and the same Act of Toleration further provided:

"Whatsoever person or persons shall from henceforth use or utter any reproachful words, or speeches, concerning the blessed Virgin Mary, the mother of our Saviour, or the holy apostles, or evangelists, or any of them, shall in such case for the first offense forfeit to the said Lord Proprietary and his heirs, the sum of five pounds sterling."— *"Proceedings and Acts of the General Assembly of Maryland, 1637-1664," p. 244.*

But those who signed the compact to qualify as citizens in Rhode Island were not asked to conform to any religious beliefs or practices, but were asked to sign the following civil covenant, the last phrase of which reveals unequivocally Roger Williams' fundamental doctrine of a complete separation of church and state, and draws a distinct and separating line between civil and religious matters as follows:

"We whose names are hereunder written, being desirous to inhabit in the town of Providence, do promise to submit ourselves in active or passive obedience to all such orders or agreements as shall be made for the public good of the body, in an orderly way, by the major consent of the present inhabitants, masters of families incorporated together into a township, and such others when they shall admit into the same only in civil things."

The last phrase, "only in civil things," was a clause of such tremendous significance that in the course of time it revolutionized the ideas of civil government, not only in America, but in many other countries of the world. Apparently it was an innocent and harmless-looking phrase with which to qualify a covenant for citizenship and the operation of a government. Most people would have read and signed such a covenant without noticing anything unusual about it, but such a doctrine in Massachusetts Bay Colony caused the banishment of Roger Williams. That doctrine was denounced as "the most damnable of heresies." Even today the advocacy of such a doctrine in some European countries still means exile or imprisonment.

Roger Williams not only wrote guaranties of religious liberty into the fundamental law of Rhode Island, but he saw that those guaranties were carried out in practice. He insisted that the civil magistrates should not sit in judgment on, or punish any man for his spiritual sins. He especially emphasized that the legislature should not enact any laws relating to the duties which a man owed to God, exclusively, nor should any man be penalized for "a breach of the first table" embodying the "first four commandments of the decalogue."

No compulsory Sunday-observance law was ever enacted in Rhode Island as long as Roger Williams was alive. The Seventh Day Baptists, who were persecuted everywhere else because they worked the first six days of the week and rested upon the seventh, were welcomed to Rhode Island, and large numbers flocked there. One of their faith

Williams Welcomes the Persecuted

In the summer of 1636 Mrs. Williams and her two small children reached Providence, and here Williams established his permanent home. He welcomed with open arms the persecuted of all faiths and all who desired freedom to worship or not to worship. Soon there were four flourishing settlements, which were formed into a confederation, or union, with Roger Williams at its head. His first concern was to make this new settlement "a shelter to persons distressed for conscience," and to establish "a civil government," which exercised authority "only in civil things." The hostile attitude toward Rhode Island on the part of the Bay Colony forced Williams to sail for England and secure a charter and protection for his newly founded colony.

finally became governor of Rhode Island. No one was barred from a civil office because of his peculiar religious faith. All citizens enjoyed equal privileges and immunities under the law. Rhode Island became the cradle of liberty in which was nurtured a model republic on democratic principles, which bloomed into full maturity in 1776 at Independence Hall in Philadelphia.

Of all men who came to America and left a lasting memorial of their work, Roger Williams holds first rank, and is often called "the first American." When the marble statue of Williams was placed in the Hall of Fame in the national Capitol building, Senator Anthony, at the dedicatory service, paid the following well-deserved tribute to this noble man:

"In all our history no name shines with a purer light than his whose memorial we have lately placed in the Capitol. In the history of all the world there is no more striking example of a man grasping a grand idea, at once, in its full proportions, in all its completeness, and carrying it out, unflinchingly, to its remotest legitimate results.

"Roger Williams did not merely lay the foundations of religious freedom, he constructed the whole edifice, in all its impregnable strength, and in all its imperishable beauty. Those who have followed him in the same spirit have not been able to add anything to the grand and simple words in which he enunciated the principle, nor to surpass him in the exact fidelity with which he reduced it to the practical business of government.

"Religious freedom, which now, by general consent, underlies the foundation principles of civilized government, was, at that time, looked upon as a wilder theory than any proposition, moral, political, or religious, that has since engaged the serious attention of mankind. It was regarded as impracticable, disorganizing, impious, and if not utterly subversive of social order, it was not so only because its manifest absurdity would prevent any serious effort to enforce it. The lightest punishment deemed due to its confessor was to drive him out into the howling wilderness. Had he not met with more Christian treatment from the savage children of the forest than he had found from 'the Lord's anointed,' he would have perished in the beginning of his experiment. . . . In his vision of the future, he saw mankind emancipated from the thralldom of priestcraft, from the blindness of bigotry, and from the cruelties of intolerance."

Roger Williams built for the future greatness of America and for the freedom of the race of mankind, and he succeeded, as few men have ever done, in his noble undertaking.

Roger Williams Dreams of Founding an Asylum for the Oppressed

While the sentence of banishment was hanging over Roger Williams' head, he saw that it was impossible to reform the existing establishments in New England, and that in order to realize his dreams it would be absolutely necessary for him to launch out into the wilderness in virgin territory and establish an asylum for the oppressed of America as well as for the persecuted in Europe. In the providence of God, Sir Henry Vane, Jr., a personal friend of Roger Williams, arrived in Salem just at this critical juncture and visited the home of Mr. Williams. Williams confided to him his contemplated dreams of establishing a new colony outside the limits of the Massachusetts Bay Colony, as well as beyond the limits of the Plymouth Colony. He was determined to frustrate the sentence of banishment back to England by

Rhode Island Erects Torch of Liberty

Roger Williams had advanced so far in "the life of love" which he advocated, and ascended so high upon the pedestal of "soul liberty" and civil and religious freedom in matters of conscience and religion, that he encountered an impossible task in his day to lift up the church-and-state leaders to his level. But the torch of liberty which he held aloft was not extinguished after his death. Other men caught the inspiration of his lofty ideals, and finally insisted that the church and the state be separated, not only in Rhode Island, but in every State in the Union. The Baptists in Virginia and elsewhere helped to make the ideals of Roger Williams the birthright of every American. May this light of religious freedom never be extinguished in America.

78

escaping into the wilds of North America. In the providence of God, and with the aid of his friends, he hoped to work out his own experiment of civil government.

Later developments indicate that Sir Henry Vane, Jr., undoubtedly promised him assistance in this contemplated experiment. His eyes turned to the uninhabited territory south of the Plymouth Colony, with which he was on terms of good friendship. He had previously visited the Indian chiefs and had done missionary work among the Narragansett Bay Indian tribes. He was confident that he could purchase land from them for his contemplated settlement. So a little more than three hundred years ago, while the sentence of banishment was waiting to be executed, Roger Williams contemplated the founding of the infant republic of Rhode Island upon the broad principles of civil and religious liberty for the enjoyment and benefit of every man, where there should exist a total separation of church and state and the equality of all religions before the civil law and the bar of justice. His hopes and dreams in due time were fully realized. His little republic became the wonder and admiration of the world and the home of the oppressed of all lands, and grew so rapidly that the Massachusetts Bay Colony became alarmed, fearing that in a few more years it would outrival the population of the older colony.

The Puritans of Massachusetts Bay Colony

thought Roger Williams was of the same spirit as they were, and that when he was powerful enough, he would retaliate for the cruel treatment they had accorded him in 1635, when they had banished him from the Bay Colony on the charge of heresy. The governor of Massachusetts, Mr. Endicott, sent two messengers to Roger Williams with a letter inviting him to join his government to the Massachusetts Bay Colony, that they might ever after live in friendly relations. But Roger Williams did not trust the Puritans of Massachusetts, and he sent the following message back to Governor Endicott: "I feel safer down here among the Christian savages along Narragansett Bay than I do among the savage Christians of Massachusetts Bay Colony."

One Great Objective

Roger Williams, after his banishment, had but one great objective to which he devoted the rest of his life, and that was to establish a government in America that might become the model for future generations, and also to create an asylum for the oppressed and persecuted of every religious faith, not only in America, but also in Europe. He believed that in order for citizens to enjoy the greatest peace and prosperity, the church and state should be entirely divorced and separated in their functions. He believed that truth was its own best defender, and that it needed neither aid from the civil government nor carnal force to advance its tenets. ("The armies of truth," he said, "like the armies of the Apocalypse, must have no sword, helmet, breastplate, shield, or horse, but what is spiritual and of a heavenly nature.")

The Puritans likewise believed in religious liberty, but they thought that this blessing should not be enjoyed by any dissenting sects which were not in agreement with the Puritan faith. In fact, the Puritans fled to America that they might enjoy the blessing of religious freedom in worship which was denied them in England before the Puritan Parliament came into supreme power under Oliver Cromwell. After the Puritans gained the ascendancy in political power in England, and even before that political upheaval, they denied to others the religious liberty which they demanded for themselves. Oliver Cromwell exposed this fault of the Puritans, of both the Presbyterians and the Independents, in a speech on the dissolution of Parliament, when he said : ("Is it ingenuous to ask liberty and not give it?) What greater hypocrisy for those who were oppressed by the bishop to become the greatest oppressors themselves so soon as their yoke was removed?"

This has ever been the case. There never yet has been a sect that has been oppressed, which, when it gained the ascendancy in numbers and strength, did not in turn oppress the weaker dissenting sects through governmental agencies and law. (It is

6

human to oppress when entrusted with power, but it is divine to grant liberty to all men, whether they agree with us or not.)

Roger Williams had caught this divine concept and principle of love, and he practiced it in his life and in his dealings with his fellow men; and the American people did well in rendering him a tardy justice and honor in the tercentenary celebration to his memory. He was in the truest sense the apostle of religious liberty to America in those turbulent and malevolent times when no man was permitted to call his faith and his soul his own. He was one hundred fifty years ahead of his day in thinking and in practicing both civil and religious liberty principles.

In fact, his ideals of total separation of church and state have never been completely carried out, even in America, in spite of our boast of religious freedom in this favored land. Our government has never divorced itself in its functions from the legal sanctions of religion and religious observances, nor from religious persecution of dissenting sects which are not in agreement with those religious legal sanctions. Full religious liberty has never yet been granted to the individual, in spite of the constitutional guaranties which vouchsafe complete religious liberty and freedom of conscience in religion.

Many of the States in the Union still have religious statutes upon their books, which have been retained from colonial times when America had a union of church and state, and these religious laws are permitted to override the Federal Constitution and its guaranties of religious liberty to the individual. All that is needed to kindle the flames of religious persecution today is to elect a religious bigot to a civil office, and these un-American laws will be invoked against the nonconformist who dares to assert the supremacy of conscience in religious matters.

The more austere and conscientious a person is in his religious convictions, the greater is the danger that he will become a persecutor of those who happen to disagree with him, provided he is entrusted with power. Like Saul the persecutor, this type of person is always actuated by the idea that in persecuting dissenters he is doing God valiant service.

The religious legalist, no matter how pious he may be, is never tolerant. Force, instead of love, is the propelling power of his religion. Everything and everybody must bow to his religious convictions. The dissenter has no right to his convictions, because he cannot be right in the sight of a self-satisfied legalist.

Roger Williams was not a legalist in religious matters. He was a dissenter, and he believed that others had the same right to dissent from his views, and that the right of dissent for all should be sacredly protected by law, so that all might stand on an equality before the bar of justice. The pages

Dissenters Fleeing to America

Dissenters and nonconformists who refused to comply with the requirements of religion as imposed by the state church were severely persecuted. While many thousands were imprisoned and punished, many more thousands fled to Holland and finally earned sufficient means to flee to America, where they had hoped they might worship God in harmony with the dictates of their own consciences. Roger Williams was one who was listed for punishment because of his opposition to Archbishop Laud's oppressive decrees. Having received a call to the pastorate of the church in Salem, he sailed with his wife on the ship "Lyon," for America. Little did he dream that he was destined to make a lasting impress upon the future of America and its institutions.

of history are stained with the blood of millions of martyrs, for the simple reason that both the church and the state failed to recognize that the right to dissent should be sacredly guarded.

As soon as Roger Williams arrived in America in 1631, he began to preach absolute liberty of religion for every sect, and for so-called heretics, and even for infidels; and he sensed that this cherished blessing for all men could never be realized without a complete separation of the church from the state. He failed, however, to convince the Puritans of Massachusetts Bay Colony. Having incurred their ill will, he was banished by them because he taught that the "civil magistrate should not punish anyone for the breach of the first four commandments" of the decalogue, or "interfere in matters of religion and conscience," nor should he "constrain anyone to this or that form of religion." Such doctrine, which at present is considered in America as sound doctrine, was then called "damnable heresy."

The banishment of Williams made him more determined than ever to plant the seeds of civil and religious liberty in America, and to found an independent government in which all could worship God in harmony with the dictates of their own conscience, in which no one could be molested by the civil magistrate so long as he conducted himself as a good citizen in purely civil matters. He decided to prepare settlements in the New World for all who were religiously oppressed in Europe as well as in America. He made his first appeal to the Independents, or Separatists, then to the Baptists and the Quakers, to come to the plantations of Rhode Island. They came from all lands in large numbers, and were granted perfect freedom of worship for all faiths. In justification of his doctrine of the absolute separation of church and state, Roger Williams said:

"The civil sword may make a nation of hypocrites and anti-Christians, but not one Christian." "Christ Jesus, the deepest politician [statesman] that ever was, . . . commands a toleration of anti-Christians." "The civil magistrates [are] bound to preserve the bodies of their subjects, not to destroy them for conscience's sake." "Seducing teachers, either pagan, Jewish, or anti-Christian, may yet be obedient subjects of the civil laws."

"Christ's lilies may flourish in His church, notwithstanding the abundance of weeds in the world permitted." "A national church [is] not instituted by Jesus Christ." "The civil commonweal, and the spiritual commonweal, the church, [are] not inconsistent, though independent the one on the other." "Forcing of men to godliness or God's worship [is] the greatest cause of the breach of the civil peace." "Masters of families, under the gospel, are not charged to force all under him from their own conscience to his." "Persons may with less sin be forced to marry whom they cannot love, than to worship when they cannot believe." ("Christ Jesus never appointed a maintenance of ministers from the unconverted and unbelieving."

Roger Williams vehemently opposed what he called "the most deplorable statute in English law," namely, the statute which compelled everybody, without distinction or religious faith, to attend the divine services in his parish every Sunday. In assailing this statute, Williams said: ("An unbelieving soul is dead in sin, and to drag an unbeliever from one form of worship to another is the same thing as changing the clothes of a corpse."

With equal earnestness he combated the practice of forced contributions for the benefit of ministers of religion. His adversaries asked: "Is not the laborer worthy of his hire?" "Yes," Williams replied, "from them that hire him, from the church."

Perhaps no sects suffered greater hardships and persecutions for their faith during the seventeenth century than the Anabaptists and the "Sabbatarian Baptists," the latter now being called "Seventh Day Baptists." Roger Williams espoused the cause of these persecuted people, and offered them an asylum in Rhode Island. In 1671 the first Sabbatarian church in America was formed in Rhode Island. Evidently this movement created a stir; for a report went over to England that the Rhode Island colony did not keep the Sabbath— meaning Sunday. Roger Williams wrote to his

friends in England denying the report, but calling
attention to the fact that there was no Scripture for
"abolishing the seventh day," and adding: "You
know yourselves do not keep the Sabbath, that is,
the seventh day."—*"Letters of Roger Williams,"
Vol. VI, p. 346. Narragansett Club Publications.*

Roger Williams not only offered the seventh-
day observers an asylum, but he championed their
cause as being the most Scriptural. Rhode Island
became the stronghold of the Seventh Day Baptist
denomination, which had large, flourishing
churches. One of their members later became a
governor of Rhode Island.

Roger Williams was truly an apostle of religious liberty sent from God to America. The
cause of religious liberty in America may still pro-
duce great leaders in defense of those fundamental
principles, but it will be difficult for any to excel
Roger Williams in the purity and logic of his
reasoning, in the breadth of conception, and in the
sincerity of the advocacy of sound principles in that
cause. Indeed, he dug diamonds in the rough out
of the mine of liberty, others polished them; he
plowed the first furrow across a virgin field, others
cultivated the plowed ground; he cut the original
pattern of liberty, others copied it; he was as a sun
shining in its meridian brightness, all others were
as satellites revolving around him.

The Principles of Religious Liberty as Conceived by Roger Williams

Roger Williams pioneered the way for the disestablishment of religion and the divorcement of the church from the state in America. The burden of his soul was that all men might be free to worship or not to worship God, as their own consciences dictated. He endeavored to reestablish primitive Christianity in harmony with the teaching and practice of the Author of Christianity. The burden of every sermon he preached, of every book he wrote, and of all his labors of charity, was to reveal the spirit of Christ to men, and lead them back to the true religion.

(He spoke and wrote of Jesus Christ as the Author of all our liberties and the Deliverer from all our bondages.) In appealing to the lawmakers and magistrates of his time to be tolerant toward all religious dissenters, Roger Williams cited the example of his Lord, saying: "Jesus Christ, the deepest politician [statesman] that ever was, . . . commands a toleration of anti-Christians." He quoted Christ as saying: "If any man hear My words, and believe not, I judge him not: for I came not to judge [condemn] the world, but to save the world. . . . The word that I have spoken, the same shall judge him in the last day." He showed that in spiritual matters God, and not man, was the judge in the last day, and therefore no man had a right to punish any man for his offenses against God and religion before the judgment day. The civil magistrates could punish men for civil offenses only —those that had to do with man's relationships to man.

He argued that it frequently happened, and was at all times possible, that "many seducing teachers, either of the paganish, Jewish, Turkish, or anti-Christian religion, may be clear and free from scandalous offences in their life, as also from disobedience to the civil laws of the state." Therefore he contended that so-called heresy should never be punished by the civil magistrate, unless the exercise of that heresy led to the violation of the rights of others, and the individual should not be punished for the heresy, but for the infringement of the rights of others.

In Roger Williams' day, every man's religion was prescribed by the state, and all had to attend church services on Sunday and give financial support to religion, whether they were members of the state church or whether they made any profession of religion. He vigorously opposed, not only compulsory church attendance on Sunday, and Sunday observance under duress of the civil magistrate, but the compulsory taxation of everybody to support religion or the state church. His ideas of a complete separation of church and state and of the free exercise of the conscience of the individual in religious matters were centuries in advance of his time. There is not a country in the world that has yet put into effect all these fundamental principles of a complete separation of church and state. Rhode Island was the only State that did it, and that State did it only as long as Roger Williams was the guiding spirit in its civil affairs. As soon as he relinquished his grip upon state affairs and passed off the stage of action, the State legislature enacted laws of religious intolerance, compelled all people to observe Sunday under the penal codes, and sent so-called heretics into exile. But as long as Roger Williams lived and had a controlling voice in the making of laws and the administration and execution of those laws, no man suffered for conscience' sake, because there were no religious laws upon the statute books under which he could be prosecuted for his dissenting views in religious matters. There can be no religious persecution when the civil government is neutral upon all religious questions.

Newgate Prison and Smithfield Plaza

Many dissenters and nonconformists were imprisoned in Newgate prison. The Quakers suffered untold hardships in this prison for their faith. Directly in front of the main entrance to Newgate prison was the Smithfield Plaza, where many sealed their fate as martyrs for their faith. Williams many times witnessed the executions and burnings of state-and-church branded heretics at Smithfield. His youthful soul was so stirred, as he saw these horrifying cruelties resulting from misunderstandings of an enforced religion, that he resolved to smite this monster of religious persecution and if possible put an end to it. He knew that the only possible way to end religious persecution was to bring about a complete separation of church and state and have religion stand on its own merits.

Roger Williams was so far in advance of the church and state leaders of his time, that to them he seemed a mere dwarf in the distance, but a consummate heretic withal. The church leaders of that day, aside from the Baptists, feared religious toleration and hated religious liberty. In following the teachings and example of John Calvin, who burned Servetus at the stake on a charge of heresy and who advocated the doctrine that "godly princes may lawfully issue edicts for compelling obstinate and rebellious persons to worship the true God and to maintain the unity of the faith," the Calvinists and Puritans did not hesitate to shed the blood of those whom they called heretics.

John Cotton not only denounced Roger Williams' views on religious freedom for the individual, but on democracy as well, saying: "Democracy, I do not conceive that ever God did ordain as a fit government either for church or for commonwealth. . . . As for monarchy and aristocracy, they are both of them clearly approved and directed in Scripture." Nathaniel Ward, who styled himself a "Lawyer Divine," and drew up the first legal code for Massachusetts Bay Colony, in replying to the argument that it was religious persecution to deprive the individual of his right to liberty of conscience in religious matters, said: "It is an astonishment to think that the brains of men should be parboiled in such impious ignorance."

Religious liberty was a perfect stranger, not only

in New England, but in every country in Europe and in every Christian denomination except the Baptists. The Protestant Reformers who had begun so nobly to proclaim the gospel of liberty, the absolute supremacy of the word of God, the separation of church and state, a full and unrestricted freedom of conscience for the individual in religious matters, and the noninterference of the state in matters of heresy, soon abandoned this exalted platform, established their own religions by law, and delivered heretics and dissenters to the state to be punished. Roger Williams, of all the great Protestant Reformers, stood alone in the integrity of his position, and finally worked out a concrete example of a free church in a free state, where no citizen was molested for holding and practicing dissenting views in religious matters. Williams never once abandoned his position on the total separation of church and state. Martin Luther, in the beginning of his Reformation work, said:

"No one can command or ought to command the soul except God, who alone can show it the way to heaven. It is futile and impossible to command, or by force to compel any man's belief. Heresy is a spiritual thing, which no iron can hew down, no fire burn, no water drown. . . Whenever the temporal power presumes to legislate for the soul, it encroaches."

But Luther compromised this principle of religious liberty when he faced an emergency and accepted aid from the state, and when he received the support of the state he robbed the great Reformation movement of the glory and splendor of a great spiritual triumph through Christ and the power of His work. His later writings reveal that he completely abandoned the principle of religious liberty and the doctrine of a separation of church and state. In writing how dissenting preachers should be dealt with, he advised:

"Since it is not good that in one parish the people should be exposed to contradictory preaching, he [the magistrate] should order to be silent whatever does not consist with the Scriptures."

Luther made his appeal to the civil ruler as the final judge and arbiter of truth, and believed that heretics should be delivered to the civil magistrate for punishment. When the Anabaptists in the lands of the Reformation taught the doctrine of immersion as the proper Scriptural mode of baptism, and proclaimed infant baptism as utterly useless and without divine authority, the great Protestant Reformers applied the whip, the sword, the torch, as well as fines, confiscation of property, and the dungeon cell to these dissenters. When the Protestant sects resorted to the civil authorities to punish heresy, it was merely a case of religious tyranny changing hands under a new religious regime.

In writing to Menius and Myconius in 1530, Martin Luther favored applying the sword to the Anabaptists. He said:

"I am pleased that you intend to publish a book against the Anabaptists as soon as possible. Since they are not only blasphemous, but also seditious men, let the sword exercise its rights over them, for it is the will of God that he shall have judgment who resisteth the power."

Melanchthon, a colaborer with Luther, in a letter to the diet at Hamburg, in 1537, advocated death by the sword to all who professed Anabaptist views. Zwingli, the Swiss Reformer, who perished with the sword, and whose statue in Zurich pictures him with a Bible in his right hand and a sword in his left, persecuted not only the Baptists, but all dissenting sects who disagreed with his views. Even John Robinson, the renowned pastor of the Pilgrims in Holland, who was far more liberal in his views than the Puritans, vigorously defended the use of the magistrate's power in matters of church discipline "to punish religious actions, he [the magistrate] being the preserver of both tables, and so to punish all breaches of both."

Roger Williams took direct issue with both the Puritans and the Pilgrims, and denied the right of the civil magistrate to legislate the first table of the decalogue into civil law or have the civil magistrate punish any of the offenses against God as set forth in the first four commandments of the law of God. It was this doctrine of the intrusion of the power of the civil magistrate into the spiritual realm, which Roger Williams so vigorously opposed, and which he fought single-handed, that caused his banishment and the bitter persecution which he had to endure everywhere in his day.

He invited the Baptists as well as the Seventh Day Baptists to come to Rhode Island, where they might enjoy their faith without civil molestation. He finally accepted their faith. He said: "I believe their practice comes nearer the practice of our great founder Jesus Christ than other practices of religion do."

When Mr. John Clarke, Mr. Obadiah Holmes, and Mr. Crandall were appointed by the Baptist church of Newport, Rhode Island, to visit an old man of the Baptist persuasion near Lynn, Massachusetts, at his own request, the civil magistrates and Puritan ecclesiastics of the Bay Colony decided it was time to nip the spread and growth of Anabaptistry in the bud. They arrested and imprisoned the three men and sentenced them to be fined or whipped. It is recorded that "they refused to pay the fines, which would be acknowledgment that they were wrong." Someone else paid Clarke's fine, without his knowledge. Mr. Holmes was whipped so severely that for a long time "he could take no rest except by supporting himself on his knees and elbows." Two of his friends, John Spur and John Hazel, who had expressed their sympathy for Mr. Holmes' pitiable condition, were arrested and imprisoned. Mr. Clarke, concerning his own trial, said:

7

Punishment for Nonconformists

The state religion prescribed every man's religion by law in Roger Williams' day. Everyone, whether a church member or not, was required to attend church services on Sunday and give financial support to the state religion. Failure to attend church services on Sunday or to pay tithes would often subject a citizen to cruel treatment and corporal punishment. Roger Williams used his voice, vote, and pen in opposing not only compulsory church attendance on Sunday, and compulsory Sunday observance under duress of the civil magistrate, but compulsory taxation of everyone to support the state religion. He drew a sharp line of demarcation between the obligations a person owed to the state "in civil things" and the duties he owed to the church and religion.

"At length the governor [John Endicott] stepped up and told us we had denied infant baptism, and being somewhat transported, told me I had deserved death, and said he would not have such trash brought into their jurisdiction."

Roger Williams wrote a letter of admonition and Christian rebuke to Governor Endicott, setting forth the great doctrine of liberty of conscience in religious matters—of the equality of all men before the law, and of the "spiritual unlawfulness of persecution for cause of conscience." In his letter to Endicott, he says:

"I speak of conscience, to persuasion fixed in the mind and heart of man. . . . This conscience is found in all mankind, more or less, in Jews, Turks, papists, Protestants, pagans, etc. . . . O, how comes it then that I have heard so often, and heard so lately, and heard so much, that he that speaks so tenderly for his own, hath yet so little respect, mercy, or pity to the like conscientious persuasions of other men? Are all the thousands of millions of millions of consciences, at home and abroad, fuel only for a prison, for a whip, for a stake, for a gallows? Are no consciences to breathe the air but such as suit and sample his?"

Again he affirmed in his letter to Endicott his well-known position, denying the right of the "magistrates dealing in matters of conscience and religion, as also of persecuting and hunting any for any matter merely spiritual and religious." He sums up the essence of his argument on liberty of conscience in the closing paragraph:

"Sir, I must be humbly bold to say that 'tis impossible for any man or men to maintain their Christ by their sword, and to worship a true Christ, to fight against all consciences opposed to theirs, and not to fight against God in some of them and to hunt after the precious life of the true Lord Jesus Christ. . . . O, remember once again (as I began), and I humbly desire to remember with you, that every gray hair now on both of our heads, is a Boanerges, a Son of Thunder, and a warning piece to prepare us for the weighing of our last anchors, and to be gone from hence as if we had never been."

Roger Williams had advanced so far in "the life of love" which he advocated, and ascended so high upon the pedestal of "soul liberty" and civil and religious freedom in matters of conscience and religion, that he encountered an impossible task to lift up the church-and-state leaders to his level. But the torch of liberty which he held aloft and which shone so brightly in Rhode Island in his day was not entirely extinguished after his death. The first Baptist church of Providence of which he was the first pastor, still voiced the message of Roger Williams, of freedom of the conscience of the individual and of the separation of church and state. The Baptists carried that message to Virginia, where they suffered much persecution; and Thomas Jefferson and James Madison became their attorneys and the defenders and champions of their cause for the disestablishment of religion. The ideas of Roger Williams found a rebirth in these two American champions of civil and religious liberty, and Thomas Jefferson gave expression to them in the Declaration of Independence, and James Madison in the Constitution of the United States.

Roger Williams conceived a republic "in civil things only" in Rhode Island, others extended it throughout the United States of America; he was the architect of a representative democracy, others followed his plans; he separated the church and the state completely, others hewed to that line of demarcation; he set the conscience of the individual above governmental authority, others maintained its supremacy; he gave us a precious heritage of civil and religious liberty, and others have merely defended and preserved it to this day. ("Roger Williams was the trail blazer for the men who framed the American Constitution.) (He made the trail which they completed and beautified as the pathway to freedom; we walk unfettered, unhindered, along this royal road. He laid the foundation for the temple of freedom which they completed and glorified; we dwell within its stately halls. He sowed the seed of liberty which brought forth a bountiful harvest; we enjoy its multiplied blessings."—*"Forty Centuries of Law and Liberty,"* by *Varner J. Johns.*

Williams and Cotton Debate Issue

The Reverend John Cotton, the self-appointed monitor of others' consciences and the spokesman of the Puritan church-and-state regime, haunted and hunted Roger Williams till he finally harried him out of the Bay Colony. But the religious controversy did not end in the exile of Roger Williams. One the champion of religious liberty, and the other the champion of religious intolerance, finally measured swords in a debate. Fortunately, this famous debate of fundamental principles and false principles of government and religion has been preserved. During this debate Roger Williams clarified and set forth the principles of religious liberty and the freedom of the conscience in religious matters and covered practically every angle of the subject.

102

The Controversy and Debate Between
Roger Williams and John Cotton

John Cotton, the son of a Puritan lawyer, was destined to become the chief antagonist of Roger Williams in the struggle over liberty of conscience in America. Mr. Cotton had been educated at Cambridge, and in his theological studies he accepted in all their fullness the theocratic principles of John Calvin, the great Genevan Reformer. Upon his arrival in Boston, he was at once called upon to direct and arrange the civil and ecclesiastical affairs of the Massachusetts Bay Colony. He at once drew up a system of laws based upon the civil and religious polity of the theocracy as established by Moses for ancient Israel.

John Cotton believed in and strongly advocated the death sentence for so-called "heretics" and for those who "seduced" souls away from the Lord

their God, and to John Cotton this meant to seduce
souls away from the Puritan faith.   As a specimen
of John Cotton's teaching upon this point, we give
the following:

"If men be found to walk in the way of the
wicked (i.e., to differ from the prevailing 'church'),
their brethren may deprive them in some cases, not
only of the common air of the country by banishment, but even of the common air of the world by
death, and yet (!) hope to live with them eternally
in the heavens.   It cannot be truly said that the
Lord Jesus never appointed the civil sword for
a remedy in such cases (heresy), for He did expressly appoint it in the Old Testament, nor did He
abrogate it in the New Testament.   The reason of
the law, which is the life of the law, is of eternal
force and equity in all ages.   Deut. 13:9.   'Thou
shalt surely kill him because he has sought to thrust
thee away from the Lord thy God.'   The reason
is of moral, therefore of universal and perpetual,
equity, to put to death the apostates, seducing
idolater or heretic who seeketh to thrust away the
souls of the people from the Lord their God."—
"Religious Liberty and the Baptists," pp. 33, 34.

This was Cotton's argument for killing heretics
and seducers of souls who led people away from the
prevailing, or state, church in his day.   It is the
same sophistry that has been employed by all heretic
hunters in all ages.   It was the identical argument
which was advanced by the Jewish rulers and

hierarchy in the days of old, against Christ Himself, and under it they secured His condemnation to death upon the cross. By the same sophistry all the apostles, with the exception of one, were condemned to die the death of heretics and seducers. It was the same argument and sophistry which decreed the death of millions of Christians in medieval times when the church and the state were united in unholy alliance. It was this bloody history that grew out of such unchristian, unholy, and unjust alliances as the result of this sophistry employed by John Cotton which led Roger Williams to expose the fallacious reasonings of Mr. Cotton, and to demonstrate through his own experiment in Rhode Island that civil government prospered and religion advanced much more rapidly when both were completely separated, and all its citizens enjoyed equal liberty of conscience, than under the old order of things.

Roger Williams took direct issue with a theocratic form of government established merely by men without a direct authority from God, and as soon as he set his foot upon American soil in Boston, he voiced his opinion that "the magistrate might not punish a breach of the Sabbath, nor any other offence," which constituted "a breach of the first table" of the decalogue. All religious laws enforced by the civil magistrate were abhorrent to the soul of Roger Williams. He was willing to give all due submission to the civil government and to the

authority of the civil magistracy in "all things
civil." He applied, as soon as he arrived in Boston, to be made a freeman. On the very day on
which Mr. Williams entered his application to
become an American citizen and a "freeman,"
the General Court of Boston, as if to challenge a
conflict at the earliest moment with Roger Williams, "ordered and agreed, that for the time to
come, no man shall be admitted to the freedom of
this body politic, but such as are members of some
of the churches within the limits of the same."

The clergy publicly and earnestly urged and
persuaded their "church members to give land to
none but such as might be fit for church members:
yea, not to receive such English into the town."

A full-fledged theocracy was set up, and for
Puritans only. They hoped to set up the kingdom
of God in America and give it to the saints only,
and only those saints who agreed with them in both
civil and religious matters. Only those were allowed to exercise the franchise. Mr. Cotton contended that " 'to erect such a government of the
church as is most agreeable to the Word,' " or in
harmony with the Mosaic theocracy, was well
pleasing in the sight of God. It was not long
before laws were enacted to banish all who refused
to conform and comply "with the state religion."

In 1644 a law was promulgated against the
Baptists, by which "it is ordered and agreed, that
if any person or persons, within this jurisdiction,

shall either openly condemn or oppose the baptizing of infants," or "seduce others or leave the congregation during the administration of the rite," they "shall be sentenced to banishment." This same year, the magistrate at the instigation of the Puritan clergy caused a poor man to be pilloried and whipped for "refusing to have his child sprinkled." Others were expatriated, and some hanged, on the charges of "heresy" and "blasphemy" because they openly expressed religious opinions contrary to those of John Cotton, the sponsor and monitor of "morals" and "religious convictions."

It was this theocratic system of government, wrought out and fathered by John Cotton, that brought Roger Williams into open conflict with this Puritan clergyman, and caused him to write his "Bloudy Tenent" against religious persecution. After Mr. Williams wrote his "Bloudy Tenent," Mr. Cotton entered into an extended debate with Mr. Williams. In this controversy between these two leaders of thought, we find the ideals and principles for which Roger Williams contended fully brought to light, and it is fortunate that history has preserved them for the benefit of American posterity who are lovers of civil and religious liberty and have a desire to preserve their heritage of freedom.

This debate between these two champions— the one advocating a union of church and state and the other an absolute separation of church and

state—is fully set forth in the "Bloudy Tenent"
and the "Bloudy Tenent Yet More Bloudy," written by Roger Williams in reply to John Cotton's
theocratic principles of government. Roger Williams ever keeps in the forefront the "sad evil," as
he calls it, which grows out "of the civil magistrates dealing in matters of conscience and religion, as also of persecuting and hunting any for
any matter merely spiritual and religious," which
led to his banishment in New England, and for
which he blamed John Cotton.

Referring to the state church of New England
as well as Old England, Roger Williams said, "I
affirm that that church estate, that religion and
worship which is commanded, or permitted to be
but one in a country, nation, or province, *that* church
is not in the nature of the particular churches of
Christ, but in the nature of a national or state
church."

Mr. Cotton held that "it is not lawful to persecute any for conscience' sake rightly informed;
for in persecuting such, Christ Himself is persecuted in them." To this argument Mr. Williams
replied: "To this distinction I dare not subscribe,
for then I should everlastingly condemn thousands,
and ten thousands, yea, the whole generation of
the righteous." "Search all scriptures, histories,
records, monuments; consult with all experiences;
did ever Pharaoh, Saul, Ahab, Jezebel, scribes and
Pharisees, the Jews, Herod, the bloody Neros,

Gardiners, Bonners, pope, or devil himself, profess to persecute the Son of God, Jesus as Jesus, Christ as Christ, without a mask or covering?

"No, saith Pharaoh, the Israelites are idle, and therefore speak they of sacrificing. David is risen up in a conspiracy against Saul; therefore persecute him. Naboth hath blasphemed God and the king; therefore stone him. Christ is a seducer of the people, a blasphemer against God, and traitor against Caesar; therefore hang Him. Christians are schismatical, factious, heretical; therefore persecute them. The devil hath deluded John Huss; therefore crown him with a paper of devils, and burn him. . . .

"And yet they say, if we had been in the days of our fathers, in Queen Mary's days, etc., we would never have consented to such persecution. And therefore, when they persecute Christ Jesus in His truths or servants, they say, 'Do not say you are persecuted for the word, for Christ's sake: for we hold it not lawful to persecute Jesus Christ.' "

Mr. Cotton further contended, " 'It is not lawful to persecute an erroneous and blind conscience, even in fundamental and weighty points, till after admonition once or twice, Titus 3:11, and then such consciences may be persecuted; . . . such a person . . . may be persecuted for sinning against his own conscience.' " Mr. Williams answered, "If persons be willfully and desperately obstinate, after light shining forth, *Let them alone,* saith the

Lord. So spake the Lord once of Ephraim: 'Ephraim is joined to idols, let him alone.' Hosea 4:17. What more lamentable condition, than when the Lord hath given a poor sinner over as a hopeless patient, incurable, which we are wont to account a sorer affliction, than if a man were torn and racked. . . . The Lord Jesus commands His servants to pass from and let alone, to permit and tolerate, when it is in their power corporally to molest them. . . . Their end is the ditch, that bottomless pit of everlasting separation from the holy and sweet presence of the Father of lights, goodness, and mercy itself. . . . I answer, the civil magistrate beareth not the sword in vain, but to cut off civil offenses, yea, and the offenders too in case. But what is this to a blind Pharisee, resisting the doctrine of Christ, who haply may be as good a subject, and as peaceable and profitable to the civil state as any: and for his spiritual offense against the Lord Jesus, in denying Him to be the true Christ, he suffereth the vengeance of a dreadful judgment, both present and eternal, as before. . . . But this sentence against him, the Lord Jesus only pronounceth. . . . Such a sentence no civil judge can pass, such a death no civil sword can inflict. . . . The great and good Physician, Christ Jesus, the Head of the body, and King of the church, hath not been unfaithful in providing spiritual antidotes and preservatives against the spiritual sickness, sores, weaknesses, dangers, of His church and people. But He never appointed the civil sword for either antidote or remedy. . . . Hence how great is the bondage, the captivity of God's own people to Babylonish or confused mixtures in worship, and unto worldly and earthly policies to uphold state religions or worships. . . . But as the civil magistrate hath his charge of the bodies and goods of the subject: so have the spiritual officers, governors, and overseers of Christ's city or kingdom, the charge of their souls, and soul safety."

Mr. Cotton replied, " 'It is a carnal and worldly, and indeed an ungodly imagination, to confine the magistrates' charge to the bodies and goods of the subject, and to exclude them from the care of their souls. . . . They may and ought to procure spiritual help to their souls, and to prevent such spiritual evils, as that the prosperity of religion amongst them might advance the prosperity of the civil state.' "

Williams answered: "If it be the magistrate's duty or office, then is he both a temporal and ecclesiastical officer: [the] contrary to which most men will affirm. And yet we know, the policy of our own land and country hath established to the kings and queens thereof the supreme heads or governors of the church of England.

"That doctrine and distinction, that a magistrate may punish a heretic civilly, will not here avail; for what is Babel, if this be not, confusedly to punish corporal or civil offenses with spiritual or church censures (the offender not being a member of it), or to punish soul or spiritual offences with corporal or temporal weapons," only "proper to delinquents against the temporal or civil state. . . . But, to see all his subjects Christians, to keep such church or Christians in the purity of worship, and see them do their duty, this belongs to the head of the body, Christ Jesus."

Mr. Cotton set forth the doctrine that the civil magistrate had a right to deal " 'with men without, as the Samaritans were, and many unconverted Christians . . . who, though carnal, yet were not convinced of the error of their way.' " Williams answered: "If the civil magistrate be a Christian, a disciple, or follower of the meek Lamb of God, he is bound to be far from destroying the bodies of men for refusing to receive the Lord Jesus Christ: for otherwise" he would "be ignorant of the sweet end of the coming of the Son of man, which was not to destroy the bodies of men, but to save both bodies and souls. . . . If the civil magistrate being a Christian, gifted, prophesy in the church (1 Cor. 14:1), . . . yet they are here forbidden to call for fire from heaven, that is, to procure or inflict any corporal judgment, upon such offenders, remembering the end of the Lord Jesus' coming [was] not to destroy men's lives, but to save them."

"True it is, the sword may make, as once the Lord complained, Isaiah 10, a whole nation of hypocrites; but to recover a soul from Satan by repentance, and to bring them from anti-Christian doctrine or worship to the doctrine or worship Christian in the least true internal or external submission, that only works the all-powerful God, by the sword of His Spirit in the hand of His spiritual officers.

"What a most woeful proof hereof have the nations of the earth given in all ages? And to seek no further than our native soil, within a few scores of years, how many wonderful changes in religion hath the whole kingdom made, according to the change of the governors thereof, in the several religions which they themselves embraced! Henry the Seventh finds and leaves the kingdom absolutely popish. Henry the Eighth casts it into a mold half popish, half Protestant. Edward the Sixth brings forth an edition all Protestant. Queen Mary within few years defaceth Edward's work, and renders the kingdom, after her grandfather Henry the Seventh's pattern, all popish. Mary's short life and religion end together; and Elizabeth reviveth her brother Edward's model, all Protestant. . . . It hath been England's sinful shame, to fashion and change their garments and religions with wondrous ease and lightness, as a higher power, a stronger sword hath prevailed; after the ancient pattern of Nebuchadnezzar's bowing the whole world in one most solemn uniformity of worship to his golden image. Daniel 3."

"A carnal weapon or sword of steel may pro-

8

Religious Freedom Versus Intolerance

Roger Williams was very apt in the use of illustrations, the same as his Master was in the use of parables to bring forcibly home to the people the true meaning of spiritual truths. The Christian was compared to an innocent lamb, and not to a ravenous wolf. Christianity was compared to the lily, and not to torments of the thornbush. The methods and means of propagating Christianity were compared to the gentle wooings of the dove, and not to seizures and ravages of the preying hawk or eagle. Williams contended that a religion that did not operate on the principle of love was not of God, but belonged to "the synagogue of Satan." True religion is distinguished by the spirit of love, and a false religion by the spirit of intolerance. Truth is its own best defender.

114

duce a carnal repentance, a show, an outside, a
uniformity, through a state or kingdom; but it hath
pleased the Father to exalt the Lord Jesus only
to be a Prince, armed with power and means sufficient *to give repentance to Israel.* Acts 5:31.

"Accordingly, an unbelieving soul being dead
in sin, although he be changed from one worship
to another, like a dead man shifted into several
changes of apparel, cannot please God. Heb. 11:6.
And consequently, whatever such an unbelieving
and unregenerate person acts in worship or religion,
it is but sin, Romans 14 [23]."

Mr. Williams contended that anything that one
man compels another to do contrary to his faith
is a sin, whether it is observing the Lord's supper,
the Lord's prayer, the Lord's baptism, or the Lord's
day; when these observances are compelled by
force, under duress of the civil magistrate, they are
"as odious as the oblation of swine's blood, a dog's
neck, or killing of a man. Isaiah 66 [3]."

"A sword of steel compels them to a worship in
hypocrisy—in the dungeons of spiritual darkness
and Satan's slavery."

"I add, that a civil sword, as woeful experience
in all ages hath proved, is so far from bringing, or
helping forward an opposite in religion to repentance, that magistrates sin grievously against the
work of God, and blood of souls, by such proceedings. Because as commonly the sufferings of false
and anti-Christian teachers harden their followers,

who being blind are by this means occasioned to tumble into the ditch of hell after their blind leaders, with more inflamed zeal of lying confidence: so, secondly, violence and a sword of steel, beget such an impression in the sufferers, that certainly they conclude, that indeed that religion cannot be true which needs such instruments of violence to uphold it; so that persecutors are far from [a] soft and gentle commiseration of the blindness of others. To this purpose it pleased the Father of spirits, of old, to constrain the emperor of Rome, Antoninus Pius, to write to all the governors of his provinces to forbear to persecute the Christians; because such dealing must needs be so far from converting the Christians from their way, that it rather begat in their minds an opinion of their cruelties."

In answering Mr. Cotton's declaration that the Christian church had a right to deliver heretics to the civil magistrates, Mr. Williams said:

"The Christian church doth not persecute; no more than a lily doth scratch the thorns, or a lamb pursue and tear the wolves, or a turtledove hunt the hawks and eagles, or a chaste and modest virgin fight and scratch like whores and harlots."

"The Christian religion may not be propagated by the civil sword."

"A false religion out of the church will not hurt the church, no more than weeds in the wilderness hurt the enclosed garden, or poison hurt the body when it is not touched or taken."

"A false religion and worship will not hurt the civil state, in case the worshippers break no civil law."

"The civil laws not being broken, civil peace is not broken."

("Heresy must be cut off with the sword of the Spirit," not "the sword of the magistrate.")

"That heresy must be cut off with the sword of the Spirit, implies an absolute sufficiency in the sword of the Spirit to cut it down, according to that mighty operation of Scriptural weapons (2 Cor. 10:4), powerfully sufficient, either to convert the heretic to God, and subdue his very thoughts into subjection to Christ, or else spiritually to slay and execute him."

In answering Mr. Cotton's argument that the Christian church was justified in employing "the civil sword" in punishing heresy, Mr. Williams replied:

"Nor could the eye of this worthy answerer ever be so obscured, as to run to a smith's shop for a sword of iron and steel to help the sword of the Spirit."

("God needeth not the help of a material sword of steel to assist the sword of the Spirit in the affairs of conscience.")

If the civil magistrate is to punish heresy, said Williams, then the officials of the civil state must be qualified with "spiritual discerning," and they "must judge and punish as they are persuaded in their own belief and conscience, be their conscience paganish, Turkish, or anti-Christian. What is this but to confound heaven and earth together, and not only to take away the being of Christianity out of the world, but to take away all civility, . . . and to lay all upon heaps of confusion?"

"The government of the civil magistrate extendeth no further than over the bodies and goods of their subjects, not over their souls."

Mr. Cotton justified his position that the Christian church had a right to punish those who sinned against their consciences by quoting Martin Luther, who said " 'that Christians sinning against light of faith and conscience, may justly be censured by the church with excommunication, and by the civil sword also, in case they shall corrupt others to the perdition of their souls.' "

Mr. Williams replied that both Cotton and Luther had gone far astray in such reasoning, and that "all persons, papist and Protestant, that are conscientious, have always suffered upon this ground especially." The denial of the right to differ, said Williams, has always been the primary cause of religious persecution.

"It is against the nature of true sheep to persecute, or hunt the beasts of the forest," said Williams; likewise the true church which is compared to sheep by nature, "does not persecute" or become "heretic hunters."

How futile is it to sit in judgment upon another's

conscience, and assume that our own way is always the true way, in the light of "the experience of our fathers' errors, our own mistakes and ignorance, the sense of our own weaknesses and blindness in the depths of the prophecies and mysteries of the kingdom of Christ, and the great professed expectation of light to come which we are not now able to comprehend," said Mr. Williams, and should not these human limitations cause us to "abate the edge, yea, sheath up the sword of persecution toward any, especially [toward] such as differ not from them in doctrines of repentance, or faith, or holiness of heart and life, and hope of glorious and eternal union to come, but only in the way and manner of the administrations of Jesus Christ."

Mr. Cotton contended that heretical teachers were "soul killers," and, therefore, were the greatest offenders against God and Christianity, and "ought to be hanged or burned."

Mr. Williams replied that "Christ Jesus hath appointed remedies sufficient in His church," through the employment of "spiritual weapons" to deal with heretics. "There comes forth a two-edged sword out of His mouth (Revelation 1 and Revelation 2), able to cut down heresy, . . . yea, and to kill the heretic: yea, and to punish his soul everlastingly, which no sword of steel can reach unto in any punishment comparable or imaginable. . . . I argue thus: the souls of all men in the world are either naturally dead in sin, or alive in Christ. If

dead in sin, no man can kill them, no more than
he can kill a dead man. . . . For the souls that are
alive in Christ, He hath graciously appointed ordinances powerfully sufficient to maintain and cher-
ish that life—armor of proof able to defend them
against men and devils.]. . .

"Grant a man to be a false teacher, a heretic,
a Balaam, a spiritual witch, a wolf, a persecutor,
breathing out blasphemies against Christ and
slaughters against His followers, as Paul did (Acts
9:1), [I say, these who appear soul killers today,
by the grace of Christ may prove, as Paul, soul-
savers tomorrow." How wrong it would have
been for the Christian church to kill Paul, when
he was "breathing out blasphemies against Christ,"]
said Williams, in reply to Cotton, and thus to have
frustrated the great soulsaving work of Paul after
his conversion. Mr. Cotton replied that Williams'
reasoning was faulty when he pleaded for the
toleration of soul killers, " 'in hope of their conversion,' " which was equivalent to proclaiming
" 'a general pardon for all malefactors; for he that
is a willful murderer and adulterer now, may come
to be converted and die a martyr hereafter.' " But
Williams countered him in this argument by claim-
ing that Mr. Cotton failed to make a distinction
between offenses against God and those against the
state. Mr. Williams contended that the civil magistrate had no right to punish a person for "soul
killing," but only for "body killing."

As soon as Roger Williams landed in Boston on his initial trip, he emphatically declared it to be his opinion that "the magistrate might not punish a breach of the Sabbath, nor any other offense, as it was a breach of the first table"—the first four commandments of the decalogue. The failure to recognize the distinction between the spiritual duties of the first four commandments of the decalogue, regulating man's relationship to God, said Roger Williams, and the secular duties of man's relationship to man as set forth in the last six commandments of the decalogue, is the primary cause of all religious persecutions.

The Sabbath of the fourth commandment is called "the Sabbath of the Lord;" it is not called the Sabbath of Caesar or the state. It belongs to God, and therefore is called "the Lord's day." Roger Williams declared that there was no more justification in enforcing the observance of "the Lord's day," by the authority of the civil magistrate, than there was of employing the civil authorities in enforcing the observance of "the Lord's supper," "the Lord's baptism," or "the Lord's prayer."

"Christ Jesus would not be pleased to make use of the civil magistrate to assist Him in His spiritual kingdom," declared Williams, "nor would He yet be daunted or discouraged in His servants by all their threats and terrors: for love is strong as death, and the coals thereof give a most vehement flame, and are not quenched by all the waters and floods of mightiest opposition."

"Christ's church is like a chaste and loving wife, in whose heart is fixed her Husband's love, who hath found the tenderness of His love toward her, and hath been made fruitful by Him, and therefore seeks she not the smiles, nor fears the frowns, of all the emperors in the world to bring her Christ unto her, or keep Him from her."

"Oh that men more prized their Maker's fear! then should they be more acquainted with their Maker's councils, for His secret is with them that fear Him."

Roger Williams claimed that the theocracy which existed back in the days of Moses and under the reigns of the kings of Israel and Judah, was terminated when God removed the crown and diadem at the time that the kings of Judah were subjected to the rule of world empires as recorded in Ezekiel 21:26, 27, " 'Thus saith Jehovah God, remove the diadem, take away the crown; this shall not be the same; exalt him that is low, and abase him that is high; I will overturn, overturn, overturn, until He come whose right it is; and I will give it Him.' " Mr. Williams contended that "the right Owner" of the crown and diadem of the God of heaven was "the Lord Jesus," and that all kings and emperors who have attempted to rule for Christ in His place on earth have worn the crown and diadem on "a usurper's head."

When "the profane, wicked prince of Israel," King Zedekiah, who was already subjected to the authority of Nebuchadnezzar, the king of Babylon, revolted against the Babylonian king, in 593 B.C., God informed the king Zedekiah that his crown and diadem would be overturned three times, successively to Medo-Persia, Greece, and Rome. After that God says: "It shall be no more, until He come whose right it is; and I will give it Him." Roger Williams understood that after the Jews rejected Christ as their King, when Pilate said to the Jews: "Behold your King;" and the Jews answered: "We have no king but Caesar," that the theocracy was abolished on the earth, and it was to be no more until Christ comes the second time on His throne of glory and then God will give it to Him.

When Mr. Cotton and the rest of the Puritan clergymen attempted to restore the ancient theocracy of Israel in New England, Roger Williams took direct issue with them and proved from the Scriptures that the theocracy was to be no more till Christ comes to reign as King of kings and Lord of lords in the world to come.

Christ has given us no "precedent," said Williams, "under the gospel, to enforce all natural and unregenerate people to acts of worship." David and Solomon, under the theocracy, said Williams, were each a king and also a prophet; "and therefore a type, as Moses also was, of that great prophet, the Son of God." But, said Williams, the kings and rulers during the Christian dispensation have been merely civil magistrates and not prophets. "But consider," said he, in reply to Cotton, who contended that civil rulers should proclaim fasts, and compel worship, "if civil powers now may judge of and determine the actions of worship proper to the saints: if they may appoint the time of the church's worship, fasting, and prayer, etc., why may they not as well forbid those times which a church of Christ shall make choice of, seeing it is a branch of the same root to forbid what liketh not, as well as to enjoin what pleaseth? . . . I know you would not take from Caesar aught, although it were to give to God; and what is God's and His people's I wish that Caesar may not take."

Mr. Cotton contended that the civil magistrate had a right to compel all people to go to church on Sunday and to other church festivals, and cited, in justification, King Josiah and "his famous acts in the church of God, concerning the worship of God, the priests, Levites, and their services, compelling the people to keep the Passover, making himself a covenant before the Lord, and compelling all that were found in Jerusalem and Benjamin to stand to it."

In reply to Mr. Cotton's citation of King Josiah for justification of what the civil magistrates were doing in New England, in compelling worshipful acts, Mr. Williams said, "Josiah was a precious branch of that royal root King David, who was immediately designed by God: and when the golden links of the royal chain broke in the usurpations of the Roman conqueror, it pleased the most wise God to send a son of David, a Son of God, to begin again that royal line, to sit upon the throne of His father David.   Luke 1:32; Acts 2:30.

"It is not so with the Gentile princes, rulers, and magistrates, whether monarchical, aristocratical, or democratical; who, though government in general be from God, yet, receive their callings, power, and authority, both kings and parliaments, mediately from the people."

"Josiah and those kings, were kings and governors over the then true and only church of God national, brought into the covenant of God in Abraham, and so downward: and they might well be forced to stand to that covenant into which, with such immediate signs and miracles, they had been brought.

"But what commission from Christ Jesus had Henry VIII, Edward VI, or any, Josiahlike, to force the many hundred thousands of English men and women, without such immediate signs and miracles that Israel had, to enter into a holy and spiritual covenant with the invisible God, the Father of spirits, or upon pain of death, as in Josiah's time, to stand to that which they never made, nor before evangelical repentance are possibly capable of?

"Now secondly, *de facto:* let it be well remembered concerning the kings of England professing reformation. The foundation of all was laid in Henry VIII. The pope challengeth to be the vicar of Christ Jesus here upon earth, to have power of reforming the church, redressing abuses, etc.: Henry VIII falls out with the pope, and challengeth that very power to himself of which he had despoiled the pope, as appears by that act of parliament establishing Henry VIII the supreme head and governor in all cases ecclesiastical, etc. It pleased the most high God to plague the pope by Henry VIII's means: but neither pope nor king can ever prove such power from Christ derived to either of them."

"An arm of flesh and sword of steel cannot reach to cut the darkness of the mind, the hardness and unbelief of the heart, and kindly operate upon the soul's affections to forsake a long-continued father's worship, and to embrace a new, though the best and truest. This work performs alone that sword out of the mouth of Christ, with two edges."

"Indeed," says Williams, "it shows a most injurious idleness and unfaithfulness in such as profess to be messengers of Christ Jesus, to cast the heaviest weight of their care upon the kings and rulers of the earth. . . . It shows abundance of carnal diffidence and distrust of the glorious power and gracious presence of the Lord Jesus, who hath given His promise and word to be with such His messengers to the end of the world."

"All true civil magistrates, have not the least inch of civil power, but what is measured out to them from the free consent of the whole: even as a committee of parliament cannot further act than the power of the house shall arm and enable them."

"If ever any in this world was able to manage both the spiritual and civil, church and commonweal, it was the Lord Jesus," declared Williams; "yet being sought for by the people to be made a king (John 6:[15]), He refused, and would not give a precedent to any king, prince, or ruler, to manage both swords, and to assume the charge of both tables" of the decalogue.

"Now concerning princes, I desire it may be remembered," said Williams, "who were most injurious and dangerous to Christianity, whether Nero, Domitian, Julian, etc., persecutors: or Constantine, Theodosius, etc., who assumed this power and authority in and over the church in spiritual things. It is confessed by the answerer and others of note, that under these latter, the church, the Christian state, religion, and worship, were most corrupted."

Williams declared that the Christian emperors, princes, and magistrates enforced the Christian religion "according to their consciences' persuasion," and forced the consciences of others, yet were not willing to be forced themselves.

Mr. Cotton claimed that the civil magistrate was under obligation as "a minister of God" to see

Religious Persuasion Versus Coercion

The real contention between Roger Williams and John Cotton in their famous debate was whether religious persuasion or religious coercion should be the controlling factor in the realm of the conscience in spiritual matters. Williams contended that the church could only use the word of God as a spiritual sword to persuade men in the domain of religion, while John Cotton attempted to justify the use of the carnal sword in correcting heretics, and the authority of the civil magistrate in disciplining church members for failure to comply with a church creed and for refusal to give financial aid to a religion that was sanctioned by the state. Williams claimed that coercion in religion could only beget meanness and hypocrisy, and would make more infidels than Christians.

that all people observed "religious ceremonies,
holy days, common prayer," and even "infant baptism," under penalty of the civil law. Mr. Williams replied that it was "a most injurious and un-
equal practice for the magistrate" to enforce by
civil authority upon dissenters, "ceremonies, holy
days, common prayer, and whatever else dislikes
their consciences, *that* the magistrate must not
bring in."

The Puritans tell the civil magistrate, said Williams, "that he is the keeper of both tables [of the
decalogue], he must see the church do her duty,
he must establish the true church, true ministry,
true ordinances, he must keep her in this purity.
Again, he must abolish superstition and punish
false churches, false ministers, even to banishment
and death."

"I confess it is most true," answered Williams,
"that no magistrate, as no other superior, is to be
obeyed in any matter displeasing to God. . . . Civil
powers may not enjoin such devices, no nor enforce
on any God's institutions, since Christ Jesus' coming." "If in matters of religion the king command what is contrary to Christ's rule, though according to his persuasion and conscience, who sees
not that . . . he ought not to be obeyed? Yea, and
(in case) boldly, with spiritual force and power,
he ought to be resisted. And if any officer of the
church of Christ shall out of baseness yield to the
command of the prince, to the danger of the church

9

and souls committed to his charge, the souls that
perish, notwithstanding the prince's command, shall
be laid to his charge. . . . According to the rule
of the Lord Jesus in the gospel, the civil magistrate
is only to attend the calling of the civil magistracy
concerning the bodies and goods of the subjects, and
is himself, if a member of the church and within,
subject to the power of the Lord Jesus therein, as
any member of the church is."

Mr. Cotton contended that " 'all magistrates
ought to be chosen out of church members,' " and
" 'that all free men elected, be only church members;' " and since " 'church members should rule,
then others should not choose, because they may
elect others beside church members.' "

Mr. Williams countered in his reply that if it
was necessary and fundamental to orderly civil
government to elect only Puritan Christians as
magistrates, how such a state of things could be
reconciled with the fact that five sixths of the
governments in the world had "never yet heard of
the name of Christ: if [therefore] their civil politics
and combinations be not lawful, because they are
not [Christian] churches and their magistrates
church members, then disorder, confusion, and all
unrighteousness is lawful and pleasing to God."

Mr. Williams also wanted to know, "since not
many wise and noble are called, but the poor receive the gospel, . . . whether it may not ordinarily
come to pass, that there may not be found in a true

church of Christ, which sometimes consisteth but of
few persons, persons fit to be either kings or governors, . . . for which services the children of God
may be no ways qualified, though otherwise excellent for the fear of God, and the knowledge and
grace of the Lord Jesus."

He also wanted to know if it was the duty of
the church "to turn the world upside down," by
turning the world out of politics, and giving politics
over to the church. This doctrine of a union of
church and state has been guilty, said Williams,
"of forcing thousands to hypocrisy in a state worship . . . of shedding the blood of such [so-called]
heretics," and "lastly, of the blood of so many hundred thousands slaughtered men, women, and children, by such uncivil and unchristian wars and
combustions about the Christian faith and religion."
"It is not the purpose of God, that the spiritual
battles of His Son shall be fought by carnal weapons
and persons. It is not His pleasure that the world
shall flame on fire with civil combustions for His
Son's sake." "The doctrine of persecution for
cause of conscience, is most evidently and lamen-
tably contrary to the doctrine of Christ Jesus, the
Prince of peace."

Mr. Cotton was responsible for the banishment
of Roger Williams at the famous trial in Salem,
when Williams had to flee into the wilderness and
almost perished for want of food, shelter, and cloth-
ing. Mr. Williams refers to a letter which he wrote

afterwards to Mr. Cotton, in which he said that if he "had perished in that sorrowful winter's flight, only the blood of Jesus Christ could have washed him from the guilt of mine." Mr. Cotton's retort was: " 'Had you perished, your blood had been on your own head; it was your sin to procure it, and your sorrow to suffer it.' "

Williams asked Cotton if it was not "a monstrous paradox, that God's children should persecute God's children, and that they that hope to live eternally together with Christ Jesus in the heavens, should not suffer each other to live in this common air together, etc. I am informed it was the speech of an honorable knight of the Parliament: 'What! Christ persecute Christ in New England?' " Mr. Cotton's retort to Williams was: " 'You have banished yourself,' " when you did not hearken "to the body of the whole church of Christ."

Mr. Williams answered that he was bound first of all to stand by God's "most holy truths,"—"only the word of Jehovah standeth fast forever;" and "I also hope, that, as I then maintained the rocky strength of them to my own and other consciences' satisfaction, so, through the Lord's assistance, I shall be ready for the same grounds not only to be bound and banished, but to die also in New England, as for most holy truths of God in Christ Jesus."

Mr. Cotton affirmed to Mr. Williams: " 'The sentence of your civil banishment ... by the magistrates . . . was neither done by my counsel nor consent.'"

Mr. Williams answered: "He publicly taught . . . that body-killing, soul-killing, and state-killing doctrine of not permitting [tolerating] but persecuting all other consciences and ways of worship but his own in the civil state, and so consequently in the whole world, if the power or empire thereof were in his hand." Moreover, said Williams, "Some that did consent [to his banishment] have solemnly testified, and with tears since to myself confessed, that they could not in their souls have been brought to have consented to the sentence, had not Mr. Cotton in private given them advice and counsel, proving it just and warrantable to their consciences. I desire to be as charitable as charity would have me, and therefore would hope that either his memory failed him, or that else he meant, that in the very time of sentence passing he neither counseled nor consented."

The particular charge that Mr. Cotton brought against Mr. Williams at the Salem trial preceding his banishment, was that Williams taught "'that the civil magistrate's power extends only to the bodies, and goods, and outward state of men,'" and did not pertain to "offenses against God and religion." This doctrine Mr. Cotton called "damnable heresy." Upon this charge, the court found Mr. Williams guilty, and pronounced him worthy of banishment. Mr. Cotton affirmed, though the magistrates rendered the judgment without his "counsel nor consent," " 'I dare not deny the sentence passed to be righteous in the eyes of God, who hath said, that *he that withholdeth the corn, which is the staff of life, from the people, the multitude shall curse him.* Prov. 11:26.' "

Mr. Williams replied that "the selling or withholding of spiritual corn, are both of a spiritual nature, and therefore must necessarily in a true parallel bear relation to a spiritual curse," and could not possibly apply to "any temporal death or banishment."

Mr. Cotton claimed that he was acting in Christ's stead: " 'Against your corrupt doctrines it pleased the Lord Jesus to fight against you, with the sword of His mouth.' " Mr. Williams replied to this charge: "I commit my cause to Him that judgeth righteously, and yet resolve to pray against their evils." "He casts dishonor upon the name of God, to make Him the author of such cruel mercy."

Mr. Williams quoted Isaiah 2:4, together with Micah 4:3, "They shall beat their swords into plowshares, and their spears into pruning hooks," and Isaiah 11:9, "There shall none hurt or destroy in all the mountain of My holiness," as proof that the Christian church was not to use carnal weapons or persecute.

Mr. Cotton replied " 'that these predictions . . . do not forbid them to drive ravenous wolves from the sheepfold, and to restrain them from devouring the sheep of Christ.'"

Mr. Williams replied: "I desire, in the fear and holy presence of God, it may be inquired into, whether in all the will or testament of Christ there be any such word of Christ, by way of command, promise, or example, countenancing the governors of the civil state to meddle with these wolves, if in civil things peaceable and obedient." "I ask, whether or no such as may hold forth other worships or religions, Jews, Turks, or anti-Christians, may not be peaceable and quiet subjects, loving and helpful neighbours, fair and just dealers, true and loyal to the civil government? It is clear they may, from all reason and experience in many flourishing cities and kingdoms of the world, and so offend not against the civil state and peace, nor incur the punishment of the civil sword, notwithstanding that in spiritual and mystical account they are ravenous and greedy wolves."

"I know that civil magistrates, in some places," said Williams, "have declined the name of head of the church, and ecclesiastical judge; yet can they not with good conscience decline the name if they do the work, and perform the office of determining and punishing a merely spiritual wolf.

"They must be sufficiently also able to judge in all spiritual causes," "who are spiritual sheep, what is their food, what their poison, what their properties, who their keepers, . . . who are wolves, what their properties, their haunts, their assaults, the manner of taking, etc., spiritually:—and this beside the care and study of the civil laws, and the discerning of his own proper civil sheep, obedient sheep, etc.: as also wolfish oppressors, etc., whom he is bound to punish and suppress. . . . And if this be not so, to wit, that magistrates must not be spiritual judges, as some decline it in the title supreme head and governor, why is Gallio wont to be exclaimed against for refusing to be a judge in such matters as concerned the Jewish worship and religion?   How is he censured for a profane person, without conscience, etc., in that he would be no judge or head? for that is all one in point of government."

Mr. Williams reminded Mr. Cotton that "the Father who gave, and the Son who keeps the sheep," are greater than all.   "Who can pluck these sheep, the elect, out of His hand?"   He further reminded Mr. Cotton that the New Testament makes it clear that "every ordinary shepherd of a flock of Christ had ability sufficient to defend the flock from spiritual and mystical wolves, without the help of the civil magistrate."

"By this unmerciful . . . most bloody doctrine, viz., the wolves (heretics) are to be driven away, their brains knocked out, and killed," that "the poor sheep to be preserved, for whom Christ died, etc.   Is not this to take Christ Jesus, and make Him a temporal king by force? John 6:15.

Is not this to make His kingdom of this world, to set up a civil and temporal Israel, to bound out new earthly, holy lands of Canaan, yea, and to set up a Spanish Inquisition in all parts of the world, to the speedy destruction of thousands, yea, of millions of souls, and the frustrating of the sweet end of the coming of the Lord Jesus, to wit, to save men's souls (and to that end not to destroy their bodies) by His own blood?"

Roger Williams quoted 2 Corinthians 10:4 against persecution: "The weapons of our warfare are not carnal, but mighty through God to the pulling down of strongholds; casting down imaginations, and every high thing that exalteth itself against the knowledge of God, and bringing into captivity every thought to the obedience of Christ; and having in a readiness to avenge all disobedience."

In interpreting this text Mr. Cotton said: " 'When Paul saith, "The weapons of our warfare are not carnal, but spiritual," he denieth not civil weapons of justice to the civil magistrate (Romans 13), but only to church officers. And yet the weapons of church officers he acknowledgeth to be such, as though they be spiritual, yet are ready to take vengeance on all disobedience (2 Cor. 10:6), which hath reference, amongst other ordinances, to the censures of the church against scandalous offenders.' "

Mr. Williams replied: "I must ask, why he

here affirmeth the apostle denies not civil weapons
of justice to the civil magistrate? of which there
is no question, unless that, according to his scope
of proving persecution for conscience, he intends
withal that the apostle denies not civil weapons of
justice to the civil magistrate in spiritual and religious causes: the contrary whereunto, the Lord
assisting, I shall evince, both from this very scripture and his own observation, and lastly by that
thirteenth of the Romans, by himself quoted.

"First, then, from this scripture and his own
observation. The weapons of church officers, saith
he, are such, which though they be spiritual, are
ready to take vengeance on all disobedience; which
hath reference, saith he, amongst other ordinances,
to the censures of the church against scandalous
offenders.

"I hence observe [according to Mr. Cotton's
view], that there being in this scripture held forth
a twofold state, a civil state and a spiritual, civil
officers and spiritual, civil weapons and spiritual
weapons, civil vengeance and punishment and a
spiritual vengeance and punishment: although the
Spirit speaks not here expressly of civil magistrates
and their civil weapons, yet, these states being of
different natures and considerations, as far differing as spirit from flesh, I first observe that civil
weapons are most improper and unfitting in matters
of the spiritual state and kingdom, though in the
civil state most proper and suitable.

"To keep to the similitude which the Spirit useth, for instance—to batter down a stronghold, high wall, fort, tower, or castle, men bring not a first or second admonition, and, after obstinacy, excommunication, which are spiritual weapons, concerning them that be in the church: nor exhortations to repent and be baptized, to believe in the Lord Jesus, etc., which are proper weapons to them that be without [the church], etc.; but to take a stronghold, men bring cannons, culverins, saker, bullets, powder, muskets, swords, pikes, etc., and these to this end are weapons effectual and proportionable. On the other side, to batter down idolatry, false worship, heresy, schism, blindness, hardness, out of the soul and spirit, it is vain, improper, and unsuitable to bring those weapons which are used by persecutors, stocks, whips, prisons, swords, gibbets, stakes, . . . but against these spiritual strongholds in the souls of men, spiritual artillery and weapons are proper, which are mighty through God to subdue and bring under the very thought to obedience. . . .

"I observe that as civil weapons are improper in this business, and never able to effect aught in the soul: so although they were proper, yet they are unnecessary. . . . Will the Lord Jesus (did He ever in His own person practice, or did He appoint to) join to His breastplate of righteousness, the breastplate of iron and steel? to the helmet of righteousness and salvation in Christ, a helmet and

crest of iron, brass, or steel? a target of wood to His
shield of faith? [to] His two-edged sword, coming
forth of the mouth of Jesus, the material sword, the
work of smiths and cutlers? or a girdle of shoe
leather to the girdle of truth? . . .

"Now, in the second place, concerning that
scripture, Romans 13, which it pleased the answerer
[Mr. Cotton] to quote, and himself, and so many
excellent servants of God have insisted upon to
prove such persecution for conscience:—how have
both he and they wrested this scripture, not as Peter
writes of the wicked, to their eternal, yet to their
own and other's temporal destruction, by civil wars
and combustions in the world? . . .

"First, then, upon the serious examination of
this whole scripture, it will appear, that from the
ninth verse of the twelfth chapter to the end of this
whole thirteenth chapter, the Spirit handles the
duties of the saints in the careful observation of the
second table [of the decalogue] in their civil conversation, or walking towards men, and speaks not
at all of any point or matter of the first table concerning the kingdom of the Lord Jesus. . . .

"From the ninth verse [of the twelfth chapter of
Romans] to the end of the thirteenth [chapter],
he plainly discourseth of their civil conversation
and walking one toward another, and with all men,
from whence he hath fair occasion to speak largely
concerning their subjection to magistrates in the
thirteenth chapter.

"Hence it is, that [at] verse 7 of this thirteenth chapter, Paul exhorts to performance of love to all men, magistrates and subjects, verses 7, 8, 'Render, therefore, to all their dues; tribute to whom tribute is due; custom to whom custom; fear to whom fear; honor to whom honor. Owe nothing to any man, but to love one another: for he that loveth another hath fulfilled the law.' . . .

"These words, 'He that loveth hath fulfilled the law,' concerneth not the whole law in the first table, that is, the worship and kingdom of God in Christ," but "of the second table. . . .

"In the ninth verse, having discoursed of the fifth command in this point of superiors, he makes all the rest of the commandments of the second table, which concern our walking with men,—viz., 'Thou shalt not kill; thou shalt not commit adultery; thou shalt not steal; thou shalt not bear false witness; thou shalt not covet: and if there be any other commandment—to be briefly comprehended in this saying, namely, thou shalt love thy neighbor as thyself.'

"And verse 10, 'Love worketh no ill to his neighbor, therefore, love is the fulfilling of the law;' that is, as before, the law concerning our civil conversation toward all men, magistrates or governors, and fellow subjects of all conditions."

John Cotton contended " 'that magistrates were keepers of the two tables, defenders of the faith against heretics.' " In answer to this argument,

Mr. Williams quoted John Calvin's comments upon Romans, the thirteenth chapter, as follows: "'But, . . . this whole discourse concerneth civil magistrates, and, therefore, in vain do they who exercise power over consciences, go about from this place to establish their sacrilegious tyranny.'"

Again Calvin says: "'Paul hath not respect unto the whole law, he speaks only of those duties which the law commands towards our neighbors.' . . . 'But Paul here only mentioneth the second table, because the question was only concerning that.' . . . 'But in that he repeateth, that love is the fulfilling of the law, understand as before, that he speaks of that part of the law which respects human society; for the first table of the law, which concerneth the worship of God, is not in the least manner here touched.'"

John Cotton retorted: "'But how far off Calvin's judgment was to restrain civil magistrates from meddling in matters of religion, let him interpret himself in his own words, in his answer to Servetus, who was put to death for his heresies at Geneva by his procurement.'" Again said Cotton: "'It was neither the word nor judgment of Calvin . . . so to interpret Romans 13, as to exempt magistrates from power of punishing heresy and idolatry.'"

Mr. Williams replied that he knew that there were some "'excellent and precious servants and witnesses of God in their times, whose names are

sweet and precious to all that fear God,—who, although their judgment ran in the common stream,
viz., "That magistrates were keepers of the two
tables, defenders of the faith against heretics,"
and' . . . suffer no other religion nor worship in
their territories, but one—their profession and practice," and "defend their faith from reproach and
blasphemy of heretics by civil weapons, and all that
from this very thirteenth of the Romans—I say, if
these particulars and others, be with fear and trem-
bling, in the presence of the Host High, examined,
the wonderful deceit of their own hearts shall appear unto them, and how guilty they will appear
to be of wresting this scripture before the tribunal of
the Most High."

John Cotton argued that Paul in the thirteenth
chapter of Romans gave the civil magistrates power
to execute vengeance, to determine which is the true
religion, and to prevent any disturbance of the true
religion by a false religion. He said, " 'In giving
them a power and charge to execute vengeance on
evildoers, it behoved them to inquire and listen
after true religion, to hear and try all, and upon
serious, deliberate, and just scrutiny, to hold fast
that which is good, and so prevent the disturbance
thereof by the contrary.' "

Mr. Williams replied that the thirteenth chapter of Romans was a strong protest "against the
use of civil weapons in matters of religions, and
spiritual worship. . . . The Spirit of God here

Endicott's Messengers to Williams

Roger Williams' commonwealth grew so rapidly for a time that Governor Endicott feared Rhode Island would soon outnumber Massachusetts, and that Roger Williams might retaliate for the wrongs they had done to him. So he dispatched two messengers to Roger Williams, proposing reconciliation and a joining of both colonies, and inviting Williams to return to Massachusetts, promising him safety. But Roger Williams did not trust the Puritans, and sent word back by the two messengers to Governor Endicott that he felt safer down among "the Christian savages" at Narragansett Bay than he did among "the savage Christians" in Massachusetts Bay Colony. He resolved to make Rhode Island a model for other governments to follow, and indeed it became a model for the American Republic.

144

commands subjection and obedience to higher powers, even to the Roman emperors and all subordinate magistrates; and yet the emperors and governors under them were strangers from the life of God in Christ, yea, most averse and opposite, yea, cruel and bloody persecutors of the name and followers of Jesus: and yet unto these, is this subjection and obedience commanded. Now true it is, that as the civil magistrate is apt not to content himself with the majesty of an earthly throne, crown, sword, scepter, but to seat himself in the throne of David in the church: so God's people, and it may be in Paul's time, . . . were apt to be much tempted to despise civil governors, especially such as were ignorant of the Son of God, and persecuted Him in His servants."

Mr. Williams contended that Paul, in the thirteenth of Romans, wrote not to the Roman governors to defend the truth and to punish heresies, because the Roman emperors and magistrates were in no way able to discern the truth, and if they were "to punish heretics, whom then also they must discern and judge, or else condemn them, as the Jews would have Pilate condemn the Lord Jesus, upon the sentence of others—I say, if Paul should have, in this scripture, put this work upon these Roman governors, and commanded the churches of Christ to have yielded subjection in any such matters, he must, in the judgment of all men, have put out the eye of faith, and reason, and sense, at once."

Mr. Williams further contended that Paul never requested the followers of Christ to submit their consciences to the Roman emperors "in spiritual things," but only "in civil things." Mr. Williams asked, if "any of the Roman governors, or the emperor himself, had been humbled and converted to Christianity by the preaching of Christ, were not they themselves bound to subject themselves unto the power of the Lord Jesus in the hands of the apostles and churches, and might not the apostles and churches have refused to have baptized, or washed them into the profession of Christ Jesus, upon the apprehension of their unworthiness?

"Or, if received into Christian fellowship, were they not to stand at the bar of the Lord Jesus in the church, concerning either their opinions or practices? were they not to be cast out and delivered unto Satan by the power of the Lord Jesus, if, after once and twice admonition, they persist obstinately, as faithfully and impartially as if they were the meanest in the empire? Yea, although the apostles, the churches, the elders, or governors thereof, were poor and mean, despised persons in civil respects, and were themselves bound to yield all faithful and loyal obedience to such emperors and governors in civil things.

"Were they not, if Christians, bound themselves to have submitted to those spiritual decrees of the apostles and elders, as well as the lowest and meanest members of Christ? Acts 16."

When Mr. Williams was asked, "Why then did Paul himself (Acts 25:11) appeal to Caesar," if Caesar was not "a fit judge" in spiritual matters? Mr. Williams replied, "I answer, if Paul, in this appeal to Caesar, had referred and submitted simply and properly the cause of Christ, his ministry and ministration, to the Roman emperor's tribunal, . . . if Paul had appealed to Caesar in spiritual respects, he had greatly profaned the holy name of God in holy things, in so improper and vain a prostitution of spiritual things to carnal and natural judgments, which are not able to comprehend spiritual matters, which are alone spiritually discerned. 1 Cor. 2:14.

"And yet Caesar, as a civil, supreme magistrate, ought to defend Paul from civil violence, and slanderous accusations about sedition, mutiny, civil disobedience, etc. And in that sense, who doubts but God's people may appeal to the Roman Caesar, an Egyptian Pharaoh, a Philistian Abimelech, an Assyrian Nebuchadnezzar, the great Mogul, Prester John, the great Turk, or an Indian Sachem?"

Mr. Cotton asserted, " 'What though the sword be of a material and civil nature? . . . It can reach to punish not only the offenders in bodily life and civil liberties, but also the offenders against spiritual life and soul liberties.' "

Mr. Williams declared that the civil magistrate "hath a sword, which he bears not in vain, delivered to him, as I acknowledge, from God's appointment in the free consent and choice of the subjects for common good.

"We must distinguish of swords. We find four sorts of swords mentioned in the New Testament.

"First, the sword of persecution, which Herod stretched forth against James. Acts 12:1, 2.

"Secondly, the sword of God's Spirit, expressly said to be the word of God. Eph. 6:[17]. . . .

"Thirdly, the great sword of war and destruction, given to him that rides that terrible red horse of war, so that he takes peace from the earth, and men kill one another. . . .

"None of these three swords are intended in this scripture. [Rom. 13:4.]

"Therefore, fourthly, there is a civil sword, called the sword of civil justice, which being of a material, civil nature, for the defense of persons, estates, families, liberties of a city or civil state, and the suppressing of uncivil or injurious persons or actions, by such civil punishment, it cannot . . . I say, cannot extend to spiritual and soul causes, spiritual and soul punishment, which belongs to that spiritual sword with two edges, the soul pierc-

(Four sorts of swords)

ing—in soulsaving, or soul killing,—the word of God."

John Cotton asked: " 'If the sword of the judge or magistrate be the sword of the Lord, why may it not be drawn forth, as well to defend His subjects in true religion, as in civil peace?' "

Mr. Williams declared: "Since the magistrates of whom Paul wrote, were natural, ungodly, persecuting, and yet lawful magistrates, and to be obeyed in all lawful civil things: since all magistrates are God's ministers, essentially civil, bounded to a civil work, with civil weapons, or instruments, and paid or rewarded with civil rewards: . . . this scripture [Rom. 13:6] is generally mistaken, and wrested from the scope of God's Spirit, and the nature of the place, and cannot truly be alleged by any for the power of the civil magistrate to be exercised in spiritual and soul matters."

Mr. Cotton contended that the kings of Israel meddled with religious matters and therefore the civil magistrates today could do the same. Said he: " 'What holy care of religion lay upon the kings of Israel in the Old Testament, the same lieth now upon Christian kings in the New Testament, to protect the same in their churches.' "

Mr. Williams declared that the kings of Israel as a general rule were "unrighteous and cruel," "fallacious," "persecuting," and "notorious evil-doers," and poor examples to follow. Said he:

"As there is a fallacious conjoining and confounding together [of] persons of several kinds and natures, differing as much as spirit and flesh, heaven and earth, each from other: so is there a silent and implicit justification of all the unrighteous and cruel proceedings of Jews and Gentiles against all the prophets of God, the Lord Jesus Himself, and all His messengers and witnesses, whom their accusers have ever so coupled and mixed with notorious evildoers and scandalous livers."

Mr. Williams stated that the kings and rulers of both the Jewish and the Christian dispensation proved themselves incompetent to judge in spiritual matters. In their judgment, for example, said Williams: "Elijah was a troubler of the state; Jeremy weakened the hand of the people; yea, Moses made the people neglect their work; the Jews built the rebellious and bad city; the three worthies regarded not the command of the king; Christ Jesus deceived the people, was a conjurer and a traitor against Caesar in being king of the Jews—indeed He was so spiritually over the Jew, the Christian—therefore, He was numbered with notorious evildoers, and nailed to the gallows between two malefactors.

("Hence Paul and all true messengers of Jesus Christ, are esteemed seducing and seditious teachers and turners of the world upside down.")

King James of England was quoted as saying

" 'that God never loves to plant His church by
blood;' " and Stephen of Poland, as saying: " 'I am
. . . a civil magistrate over the bodies of men, not
a spiritual over their souls;' " and the king of
Bohemia, as saying: " 'That conscience ought not
to be violated or forced. . . . That persecution for
cause of conscience hath ever proved pernicious,
being the causes of all those wonderful innovations
of, or changes in, the principalest and mightiest
kingdoms of Christendom.' "

Mr. Cotton replied to this: " 'For those three
princes named by you, who tolerated religion, we
can name you more and greater who have not tolerated heretics and schismatics, notwithstanding their
pretense of conscience.' "   Then Mr. Cotton pro-
ceeds to name a large number of notable kings,
emperors, and queens of "greater piety" who would
not tolerate heresy or schism.

Mr. Cotton said: " 'Constantine the Great at
the request of the general council of Nice, banished
Arius, with some of his fellows. . . .

" 'The same Constantine made a severe law
against the Donatists: and the like proceedings
against them were used by Valentinian, Gratian,
and Theodosius, as Augustine reports. . . . Only
Julian the Apostate granted liberty to heretics as
well as to pagans. . . .

" 'Queen Elizabeth, as famous for her government as most of the former, it is well known what
laws she made and executed against papists. Yea,

and King James, one of your own witnesses, though
he was slow in proceeding against papists, as you
say, for conscience' sake, yet you are not ignorant
how sharply and severely he punished those whom
the malignant world calls Puritans, men of more
conscience and better faith than the papists whom
he tolerated.' "

Mr. Williams in reply said: "Unto this, I answer: First, that for mine own part I would not
use an argument from the number of princes,
witnessing in profession of practice against persecution for cause of conscience; for the truth and
faith of the Lord Jesus must not be received with
respect of faces, be they never so high, princely and
glorious.

"Precious pearls and jewels, and far more
precious truth, are found in muddy shells and
places.   The rich mines of golden truth lie hid
under barren hills, and in obscure holes and corners.

"The most high and glorious God hath chosen
the poor of the world, and the witnesses of truth
(Revelation 11) are clothed in sackcloth, not in
silk or satin, cloth of gold or tissue: and, therefore,
I acknowledge, if the number of princes professing
persecution be considered, it is rare to find a king,
prince, or governor like Christ Jesus, the King of
kings, and Prince of the princes of the earth, and
who tread not in the steps of Herod the fox, or
Nero the lion, openly or secretly persecuting the
name of the Lord Jesus; such were Saul, Jereboam.

Ahab, though under a mask or pretense of the name
of the God of Israel.

"To that purpose was it a noble speech of Buchanan, who, lying on his deathbed, sent this item
to King James:—'Remember my humble service
to His Majesty, and tell him that Buchanan is
going to a place where few kings come.'"

Mr. Williams further stated that Mr. Cotton
himself admitted "'that amongst the Roman emperors, they that did not persecute were Julian the
Apostate, and Valens the Arian; whereas the good
emperors, Constantine, Gratian, Valentinian, and
Theodosius, they did persecute the Arians, Donatists,' etc."

To this argument Mr. Williams replied: "It is
no new thing for godly, and eminently godly men
to perform ungodly actions: nor for ungodly persons, for wicked ends, to act what in itself is good
and righteous."

Mr. Williams then cited as examples such great
and holy men as Abraham, Jacob, David, Solomon,
Lamech, and Saul, all of whom "lived in constant
transgression against the institution of so holy and
so ratified a law of marriage," and "other sins are
wont to be recorded of them."

Mr. Williams argued that it was not safe to look
to men or the examples of men, no matter how
eminent they were, that Christ was the only pattern
we must follow. Though King David ordered
the "slaughter of Uriah," he afterward repented and

sought God's forgiveness, and thus "David was holy and precious to God still, though like a jewel fallen into the dirt. Whereas King Ahab, though acting his fasting and humiliation, was but Ahab still."

Mr. Williams said the misguided "zeal of Constantine and other emperors, did more hurt to Christ Jesus' crown and kingdom, than the raging fury of the most bloody Neros. In the persecutions of the latter, Christians were sweet and fragrant, like spice pounded and beaten in mortars. But these good emperors, persecuting some erroneous persons, Arius, etc., and advancing the professors of some truths of Christ—for there was no small number of truths lost in those times—and maintaining their religion by the material sword—I say, by this means Christianity was eclipsed, and the professors of it fell asleep (Cant. 5:2), Babel, or confusion, was ushered in, and by degrees the gardens of the churches of saints were turned into the wilderness of whole nations, until the whole world became Christian, or Christendom. Revelation 12, 13.

"Doubtless those holy men, emperors and bishops, intended and aimed right to exalt Christ; but not attending to the command of Christ Jesus, to permit the tares to grow in the field of the world, they make the garden of the church and field of the world to be all one; and might not only sometimes, in their zealous mistakes, persecute good wheat instead of tares, but also pluck up thousands of those precious stalks by commotions and combustions about religion, as hath been since practiced in the great and wonderful changes wrought by such wars in many great and mighty states and kingdoms, as we heard even now in the observation of the king of Bohemia. . . .

"This is the common clamor of persecutors against the messengers and witnesses of Jesus in all ages," said Williams, "viz., you are heretics, schismatics, factious, seditious, rebellious. Have not all truth's witnesses heard such reproaches? You pretend conscience: you say you are persecuted for religion: you will say you are martyrs? . . . Doubtless, that soul that can so readily speak Babel's language, hath cause to fear that he hath not yet in point of worship left the gates or suburbs of it."

Mr. Cotton declared that when Julian the Apostate and Valens the Arian tolerated " 'all weeds to grow,' " it was " 'that thereby they might choke the vitals of Christianity.' "

Mr. Williams replied: "When Christianity began to be choked, it was not when Christians lodged in cold prisons, but down beds of ease, and persecuted others."

Mr. Williams declared that Mr. Cotton concluded his argument "with approbation of Queen Elizabeth for persecuting the papists, and a reproof to King James for his persecuting the Puritans." "I answer," said Mr. Williams, "if Queen Eliza-

beth, according to the answerer's [Mr. Cotton's]
tenent and conscience, did well to persecute according to her conscience, King James did not ill in
persecuting according to his. For Mr. Cotton must
grant that either King James was not fit to be a
king, had not the essential qualifications of a king,
in not being able rightly to judge who ought to be
persecuted, and who not: or else he must confess
that King James, and all magistrates, must persecute such whom in their conscience they judge
worthy to be persecuted."

Mr. Cotton replied: " 'It followeth not. For
Queen Elizabeth might do well in persecuting
seditious or seducing papists, according to conscience rightly informed, and King James do ill
according to conscience misinformed.' "

Mr. Williams stated his position thus: "I say
it again, though I neither approve Queen Elizabeth
or King James in such their persecutions, yet such
as hold this tenent of persecuting for conscience,
must also hold that civil magistrates are not essentially fitted and qualified for their function and
office, except they can discern clearly the difference
between such as are to be punished and persecuted,
and such as are not.

"Or else, if they be essentially qualified, without such a religious spirit of discerning, and yet
must persecute the heretic, the schismatic, etc.,
must they not persecute according to their con-

sciences and persuasion? And then doubtless, though he be excellent for civil government, may he easily, as Paul did ignorantly, persecute the Son of God instead of the son of perdition.

"Therefore, lastly, according to Christ Jesus' command, magistrates are bound not to persecute, and to see that none of their subjects be persecuted and oppressed for their conscience and worship, being otherwise subject and peaceable in civil obedience."

Mr. Cotton justified "the persecution of the papists by Queen Elizabeth," and similar persecution of the papists "in the Low Countries," or the Netherlands, because the " 'Duke D'Alva boasts that 36,000 Protestants were put to death by him,' " for which " 'the Jesuits' " were responsible, and therefore, says Cotton, the Protestants were justified in banishing the Jesuits from the country in 1586. Mr. Cotton said: " 'They [the Protestants] justly say Amen to the queen's law—that as she gave the popish emissaries blood to drink—the angel says, "Even so, Amen" [Rev. 16:7]. They acknowledge God's almighty power, that had given them power to make that law against them—"all states rang of these laws, and it raised all Christendom" ' " " 'in combustion; raised the wars of 1588 and the Spanish invasion,' " and he adds, both concerning the English nation and the Dutch, " 'that if God had not borne witness to His people and their laws, in defeating the intendments of their enemies, against both nations, it might have been the ruin of them both.' "

Mr. Williams replied: "That those laws and practices of Queen Elizabeth raised those combustions in Christendom, I deny not: that they might likely have cost the ruin of English and Dutch, I grant.

"That it was God's gracious work in defeating the intendments of their enemies, I thankfully acknowledge. But that God bore witness to such persecutions and laws for such persecutions, I deny: for, First, event and success come alike to all, and are no argument of love, or hatred, etc.

"Secondly, the papists in their wars have ever yet had, both in peace and war, victory and dominion; and therefore, if success be the measure, God hath borne witness unto them.

"It is most true, what Daniel in his eighth, and eleventh, and twelfth chapters, and John in his Revelation, eleventh, twelfth, and thirteenth chapters, write of the great success of antichrist against Christ Jesus for a time appointed.

"Success was various between Charles V and some German princes: Philip of Spain and the Low Countries; the French king and his Protestant subjects; sometimes losing, sometimes winning, interchangeably.

"But most memorable is the famous history of the Waldenses and Albigenses, those famous wit-

nesses of Jesus Christ, who rising from Waldo, at
Lyons in France (1160), spread over France, Italy,
Germany, and almost all countries, into thousands
and ten thousands, making separation from the pope
and Church of Rome. These fought many battles
with various success, and had the assistance and
protection of divers great princes against three
succeeding popes and their armies; but after mutual
slaughters and miseries to both sides, the final success of victory fell to the popedom and Romish
church, in the utter extirpation of those famous
Waldensian witnesses.

"God's servants are all overcomers when they
war with God's weapons, in God's cause and worship: and in Revelation second and third chapters,
seven times it is recorded—'To him that overcometh,' in Ephesus; 'to him that overcometh,' in
Sardis, etc.; and Revelation twelfth, God's servants
overcame the dragon, or devil, in the Roman emperors by three weapons—the blood of the Lamb,
the word of their testimony, and the not loving of
their lives unto the death."

Mr. Cotton said he was willing to admit that
" 'the Christian church doth not persecute, but is
persecuted. But,' " said Mr. Cotton, " 'to excommunicate a heretic, is not to persecute, that is, it is
not to punish an innocent but a culpable and damnable person, and that not for conscience, but for
persisting in error against light of conscience,
whereof he hath been convinced.' "

Mr. Williams replied: "I answer, If it be a mark of the Christian church to be persecuted, and of the anti-Christian, or false church, to persecute, then those churches cannot be truly Christian, according to the first institution, which either actually themselves, or by the civil power of kings and princes given to them, or procured by them to fight for them, do persecute such as dissent from them, or be opposite against them."

Mr. Williams added if " 'to excommunicate a heretic is not to persecute, but to punish him for sinning against the light of his own conscience,' " as Mr. Cotton asserted, then, said Williams, Mr. Cotton must make a distinction between what is "spiritual" and what is "civil." "Excommunication being of a spiritual nature . . . and a spiritual killing by the most sharp two-edged sword of the Spirit, in delivering up the person excommunicated to Satan—therefore, who sees not that his answer comes not near our question?"

Mr. Williams said it was one thing for the church to excommunicate its own members "in spiritual and church matters" and by spiritual excommunications, but it was an entirely different thing to punish "a heretic for sinning against his conscience," "by imprisonments, stocking, whipping, fining, banishing, hanging, burning, etc., notwithstanding that such persons in civil obedience and subjection are unreprovable."

"I conclude," said Mr. Williams, "THAT THE CHRISTIAN CHURCH DOTH NOT PERSECUTE; NO MORE THAN A LILY DOTH SCRATCH THE THORNS, OR A LAMB PURSUE AND TEAR THE WOLVES, OR A TURTLEDOVE HUNT THE HAWKS AND EAGLES, OR A CHASTE AND MODEST VIRGIN FIGHT AND SCRATCH LIKE WHORES AND HARLOTS. . . . THE CHRISTIAN RELIGION MAY NOT BE PROPAGATED BY THE CIVIL SWORD."

AMEN

11

Williams—the Peacemaker

After all his mistreatment at the hands of the Massachusetts Bay Colony, Williams, at the risk of his life, visited the hostile Indian camps and interceded with the Indian chiefs who had determined to wipe the Massachusetts Bay Colony completely out of existence. At the moment the Indians were ready to strike the annihilating blow, Roger Williams walked into the midst of the Indian camp, with guns and arrows pointed at him from every angle, and begged the Indian chiefs to listen to him. He succeeded in getting them to postpone the planned attack until his interview was concluded. He labored days and nights before he finally succeeded in obtaining the consent of the Indian chiefs to arbitrate the matter. Thus he again saved the lives and homes of his former persecutors.

162

Roger Williams : The Peacemaker

Roger Williams was not only a pioneer in religious liberty ideals and principles far in advance of his time, but he was unexcelled in his day as a peacemaker. He lived in stormy times, and the settlers in New England were in constant danger of attack from the savage Indians, as well as from jealous and rival factions of white men. He not only served as an efficient peacemaker between the various factions whose political aggrandizements threatened to destroy each other, but he was able to calm the ferocity of rival Indian tribes against each other as well as against his enemy, the Massachusetts Bay Colony, on whose destruction the Indians had determined.

Roger Williams had a pleasing personality and the happy faculty of bringing order out of chaos. After he left on his second trip to England to make the charter of Rhode Island more secure against Puritan encroachment from Massachusetts than it was as it was first drawn, some heated jealousies sprang up between the various plantations of Rhode Island. Roger Williams induced his old friend, Sir Henry Vane, to write a letter addressed to the inhabitants of the colony of Rhode Island, deprecating the divisions among them, "the headiness, tumults, disorders, injustice," "the noise [of which] echoes into the ears of all, as well friends as enemies, by every return of ships" from New England. He pleaded with them:

"Is not the love of Christ in you, to fill you with yearning bowels, one towards another, and constrain you not to live to yourselves, but to Him that died for you, yea, and is risen again? Are there no wise men amongst you? No public self-denying spirits, that at least, upon the grounds of common safety, equity, and prudence, can find out some way or means of union and reconciliation for you amongst yourselves, before you become a prey to common enemies?"

He further suggested that they choose "commissioners agreed on and appointed in all parts, and on behalf of all interests," to effect, "in a general meeting," such a union and common satisfaction as might put a stop to their growing "breaches and distractions," silence their enemies, encourage their friends, honor the name of God, and refresh and revive his sad heart, their affectionate friend— Roger Williams.

When Roger Williams finally returned from England in August, 1654, he found the various towns and plantations so hopelessly divided and in civil strife with one another that it taxed his skill and ingenuity to the utmost to effect a reconciliation between the warring factions. He addressed a strong appeal to his "well-beloved friends and neighbors," which not only reflects the utter confusion, the jealousies, and the petty and senseless wrangling of the townsmen, but also reveals his unexcelled qualities as a leader and peacemaker. He told them how he had "spent almost five years with the state of England, to keep off the rage of the English against us," and how he had labored incessantly "to keep up the name of a people, a free people, not enslaved to the bondages and iron yokes of the great oppressions of the English and barbarians about us," and all the reward he had obtained for this service was "grief and sorrow and bitterness." He further stated, "I have been charged with folly for that freedom and liberty which I have always stood for; I say, liberty and equality, both in land and government. . . . But, gentlemen, blessed be God who faileth not, and blessed be His name for His wonderful providences, by which alone this town and colony, and that grand cause of truth and freedom of conscience, hath been upheld to this day."

The deputies of the different plantations had refused to come to the general assembly in Provi-

dence or to meet together in conference to iron out
their differences, and their union was on the point
of dissolution and likely to be swallowed up by the
Massachusetts Bay Colony. Roger Williams dis-
played his qualities as a leader of opposing factions
at this critical moment, and took personal respon-
sibility in effecting peace and harmony. He promised all deputies of every faction, if they came
together to consider "the common peace, and common safety, and common credit," and were willing
to sacrifice something for the cause of "pacification"
and "for a union" of the plantations, that all should
have the right of "free debate and conference" and
the right to "vote in all matters with us" of the
plantations.

This appeal had its inevitable effect, and prepared the way for the reconvening of the General
Assembly in Providence and the reconciling of all
their differences, and led not only to the reestablish-
ment of the union, but to the making of the Union
of the Providence Plantations more democratic.
At a general election held on September 12, 1654,
Roger Williams was elected president of the Republic of the Providence Plantations. Though this
choice of the people of Rhode Island was quite contrary to his own choice and wish, yet the public
need and demand, as in the case of George Washington in his election to the first Presidency of the
Republic of the United States, made his acceptance
of the office inevitable.

The General Assembly, which ratified the election of Roger Williams as president, authorized him to write a letter of thanks to His Highness the Lord Protector, Oliver Cromwell, and to Sir Henry Vane and other friends in England, in the name of the republic of the Providence Plantations, and that Mr. Roger Williams subscribe his name "with the title of his office."

The people of Rhode Island were proud of the new form of their government, and they were proud of their first president, who had set up a model republic, as a pattern for others to follow, with the church and state completely separated, with the conscience of the individual unfettered in religious matters, with the franchise granted to all citizens, with freedom of the press and of speech granted to all men, and with rulers and lawmakers selected only by the consent of the governed.

In writing this letter of "humble thanksgiving" to Sir Henry Vane, the first president of this miniature republic in America referred with gratitude to "the many providences of the Most High, toward this town of Providence, and this Providence Colony," and to the many letters Sir Henry Vane had directed to the inhabitants of Rhode Island who had been "an outcast and despised people. From the first beginning of this Providence Colony (occasioned by the banishment of some in this place from the Massachusetts) we say, ever since, to this very day, we have reaped the sweet fruits

Williams—the Arbitrator

While Williams was in England endeavoring to secure a charter from Parliament to make the liberties in Rhode Island secure, and preventing the New England confederacy from absorbing Rhode Island, the four Plantations were on the verge of each going their own way and dissolving the union because of irreconcilable disagreements. Williams hastened back home to effect a peaceable reconciliation. In May, 1647, he succeeded in reuniting them, when the General Assembly of Rhode Island adopted a code of laws which contained the declaration, "All men may walk as their consciences persuade them, without molestation—every one in the name of his God"—full and complete religious liberty to "all men." Any nation with such ideals is bound to be exalted.

of your constant loving-kindness and favor toward us."

He continued to express his gratitude for their deliverance from the oppressions and persecutions under which the people of Europe were still suffering and for the great liberties which they were now enjoying, saying:

"We have long drunk of the cup of as great liberties as any people that we can hear of under the whole heaven. We have not only been long free . . . from the iron yoke of wolfish bishops, and their popish ceremonies (against whose cruel oppressions God raised up your noble spirit in Parliament), but we have sitten quiet and dry from the streams of blood spilt by that war in our native country. We have not felt the new chains of the Presbyterian tyrants, nor in this colony have we been consumed with the overzealous fire of the (so-called) godly Christian magistrates.

"Sir, we have not known what an excise means; we have almost forgotten what tithes are, yea, or taxes either, to church or commonwealth. We could name other special privileges, ingredients of our sweet cup, which your great wisdom knows to be very powerful . . . to render the best of men wanton and forgetful. . . . We hope you shall no more complain of the saddening of your loving heart by the men of Providence Town or Providence Colony, but that when we are gone and rotten, our posterity and children after us shall

read in our town records your pious and favorable letters, and loving-kindness to us, and this our
answer and real endeavor after peace and righteousness."

But no sooner had Roger Williams settled
peaceably the internal dissensions of the Providence
Colony than his ingenuity was taxed to the utmost
to placate and pacify the external threatenings of
another Indian war proposed by Massachusetts
against the Narragansets. As peacemaker he be-
stirred himself to prevent the conflict. He reminded the General Court of Massachusetts, which
proposed another war against the Narraganset Indians, that in the Pequot wars he was appointed
by their government to the hazardous and weighty
service and mission of negotiating a league of peace
between themselves and the Narragansets, to the
imminent danger of his own life at the hands of
the Pequot messengers in the Narraganset camp;
and that when he had succeeded in arbitrating their
differences and effecting a league of peace, their
government had been pleased to send him a copy
of the league, subscribed by all hands there; and
that "since that time in all their great transactions
of war and peace between the English and the
natives, he had not spared purse, nor pains, nor
hazards, very many times, that the whole land might
sleep in peace securely;" and that he would not be
doing his duty to the Parliament of England, the
Council of State, and His Highness the Protector,

if he should be silent, when their mutual interests were "not a little concerned in the peace or war" of New England, and since "among their other favors to the colony of Providence Plantations, some were expressly concerning these very Narraganset Indians, the native inhabitants of this jurisdiction."

While Roger Williams worked for peace by means of arbitration, yet he was not a pacifist who would never justify the use of the sword. He earnestly declared to the General Court of Massachusetts that he was "never against the righteous use of the civil sword of men or nations, but yet, since all men of prudence, ply to windward to maintain their wars to be defensive," then he earnestly pleaded with his Massachusetts brethren "to live and die in peace with all the natives of New England."

"Secondly," he wrote, "are not all the English of this land, generally, a persecuted people from their native soil? And hath not the God of peace and Father of mercies made these natives more friendly in this, than our native countrymen in our own land, to us? Have they not entered leagues of love, and to this day continued peaceable commerce with us? Are not our families grown up in peace among them? Upon which I humbly ask, How can it suit with Christian ingenuity to take hold of some seeming occasions for their destruction, which, though the heads be only aimed at, yet all experience tells us, falls on the body and the innocent?"

Again Roger Williams succeeded, as he had upon numerous occasions before, in averting a general war with the Narragansets. He was the peacemaker of New England. Through his indefatigable efforts of charity, he reconciled his enemies with their enemies. The charity he possessed was the charity of Christ, which led him to forgive his enemies as Christ forgave His. At the risk of his own life he saved Puritan and Pilgrim alike from impending Indian massacres, even though they had exiled him to the wilderness and suffering. His spirit of love and liberty for all men, irrespective of their divergent beliefs, enabled him to win men to his standard and to form an enduring compact binding men together in the bond of political union "only in civil things." These United States are the fruition of his hopes, his faith, his ideals, and his labors. All honor to the ideals, the faith, the hope, and the charity of Roger Williams; but the greatest of those was his charity for his enemies, even though they did not appreciate his efforts.

THE PEACEMAKER

THE PRESENT CRISIS

Once to every man and nation comes the moment to decide,
In the strife of truth with falsehood, for the good or evil side;
Some great cause, God's new Messiah, offering each the bloom
    or blight,
Parts the goats upon the left hand, and the sheep upon the right,
And the choice goes by forever 'twixt that darkness and that
    light.

       .   .   .   .

Then to side with truth is noble when we share her wretched
    crust,
Ere her cause bring fame and profit, and 'tis prosperous to be
    just;
Then it is the brave man chooses, while the coward stands aside,
Doubting in his abject spirit, till his Lord is crucified,
And the multitude make virtue of the faith they had denied

       .   .   .   .

For Humanity sweeps onward: where today the martyr stands,
On the morrow crouches Judas with the silver in his hands;
Far in front the cross stands ready and the crackling fagots
    burn,
While the hooting mob of yesterday in silent awe return
To glean up the scattered ashes into history's golden urn.

       .   .   .   .

New occasions teach new duties; time makes ancient good un-
    couth;
They must upward still, and onward, who would keep abreast
    of truth;
Lo, before us gleam her campfires! we ourselves must Pilgrims
    be,
Launch our Mayflower, and steer boldly through the desperate
    winter sea,
Nor attempt the future's portal with the past's blood-rusted key.
               —*James Russell Lowell.*

Sparks From the Editor's Anvil*

THE best test of genuine religion is its ability to stand on its own merits.

The man who has the greatest charity for man, serves God the best.

True religion never knocks at the door of Caesar's chamber for legislative sanction.

Truth never asks for legal aid, only for a fair field in its contest with error.

A legal religion will never supply the lack of moral backbone.

If government is to keep out of the realm of religion, the church must keep out of the arena of politics.

The free exercise of a natural right never injures anyone, nor does it do violence to morality.

Ambition becomes a deadly enemy when it leads a man to trample upon the rights of others to raise himself into power.

The preacher who makes his religion legalistic, makes it repulsive; he who makes it inspirational, makes it attractive.

God never made any man great enough, good enough, or wise enough to sit in judgment upon the motives of another man.

* These "Sparks" are taken from the *Liberty* magazine, published in Washington, D.C., of which the author of this book for the last twenty-eight years has been editor.

174

Roger Williams: The Stalwart Idealist

It was fortunate for America that Roger Williams was banished from England by untoward circumstances, and from the Puritan colony by a general court action. Had he not experienced these hardships as a result of a church-and-state union, he might never have seen the clear light of religious liberty in all its fullness nor remained steadfast as its defender to the end of his career. He had tasted the bitter dregs of religious persecution and witnessed the baneful results of a denial of human rights. He saw and experienced all the evil consequence of religious legislation and also of the interference of the civil magistrate in matters of conscience in the prescription and enforcement of religious obligations.

He also lived long enough to see his own experiment of a complete separation of church and

175

state develop into the fruition of his brightest hopes. He had the good fortune to found a new government in a wilderness previously unoccupied except by roaming Indians, from whom he purchased the land. There were no cherished traditions or legal precedents from a former administration of government handed down to handicap his new experiment. He had the privilege and unprecedented opportunity to build a republic and create and mold it in harmony with his own ideals.

A kind Providence prolonged his days, enabling him to perfect his scheme and to demonstrate that a government of the people, by the people, and for the people, under a complete separation of church and state, produced the happiest results in society that the world has yet witnessed in any human government on earth. He demonstrated that religion prospered best without state aid and without legal sanctions.

Williams was so gratified with the beneficent results of his new experiment in liberating the conscience of the individual and in safeguarding that precious heritage in constitutional law which he was handing down to his successors, that he admonished them with these burning words to preserve this priceless legacy: ("Having bought the truth dear, we must not sell it cheap; not the least grain of it for the whole world.")

Roger Williams, as a sound-minded and well-seasoned statesman, steadfastly protested to the closing days of his life that "the civil magistrate ought not to punish a breach of the first table of the law, comprised in the first four of the ten commandments." He never receded from his position that the compulsory Sunday-observance laws enacted by the Puritans and the Pilgrims of New England were all wrong and entirely foreign to the gospel plan.

The observance of the first four commandments of the decalogue, he held, were duties which man owed exclusively to God, and as such did not fall within the civil duties which man owed to the state. He was confident that God purposely wrote the ten commandments upon two separate tables of stone in order to separate the duties and obligations which were purely religious and spiritual from those which were also secular and civil. He was positively certain that if the civil magistrate recognized this distinction between the religious aspects of the first table of the decalogue and the civil nature of the second table, and refused to enforce the first four commandments, it would lead to the total separation of church and state, and make religious persecution impossible.

A kind Providence permitted him to be banished from the Massachusetts Bay Colony, where it was impossible for him to work out his experiment, and opened an effectual door for him in Rhode Island to perfect his plans of a truly civil government. Here he realized his ideals and saw

First and Second Tables Distinguished

Roger Williams in all his teachings drew a sharp distinction between the first and second tables of the decalogue. He took issue with the Puritans and the Pilgrims when they attempted to enforce the first four commandments of the decalogue. He claimed that they were clearly spiritual requirements which a man owed directly to God and not to Caesar. He contended that Sabbath observance was spiritual, and that a breach of the Sabbath, or Sunday observance likewise, should never be enforced by the civil magistrate or under the penal codes. Because of his opposition to their compulsory Sunday laws and many other religious requirements, he had to suffer bitter persecution. He never yielded one iota on the complete separation of church and state.

178

"mankind emancipated from the thralldom of priestcraft, from the blindness of bigotry, from the cruelties of intolerance. He saw the nations walking forth in the liberty wherewith Christ had made them free."

The learned German historian Gervinus said of Williams that he founded a "new society in Rhode Island upon the principles of entire liberty of conscience, and the uncontrolled power of the majority in secular concerns, . . . [which principles] have not only maintained themselves here, but have spread over the whole union, . . . [and] given laws to one quarter of the globe; and, dreaded for their moral influence, they stand in the background of every democratic struggle in Europe."

When Roger Williams was accused of sustaining anarchy by his liberal views, and thereby distorting civil government and hindering the progress of Christianity, he wrote his immortal essay on the question, which has been considered an imperishable classic. Among the many wise and good things, he said:

"There goes many a ship to sea, with many hundred souls on one ship, whose weal and woe is common, and is a true picture of a commonwealth, or a human combination or society. It hath fallen out sometimes that both papists and Protestants, Jews and Turks, may be embarked into one ship; upon which supposal I [do] affirm that all the liberty of conscience that ever I pleaded for turns upon these two hinges; that none of the papists, Protestants, Jews, or Turks be forced to come to the ship's prayers or worship; nor [secondly] compelled from their own particular prayers or worship if they practice any.

"I further add, that I never denied, that notwithstanding this liberty, the commander of this ship ought to command the ship's course, yea, and also command that justice, peace, and sobriety be kept and practiced both among the seamen and all the passengers. If any of the seamen refuse to perform their service, or passengers to pay their freight; if any refuse to help, in person or purse, towards the common charges or defense; if any refuse to obey the common laws and orders of the ship concerning their common peace or preservation; if any shall mutiny and rise up against their commanders and officers; if any should [shall] preach or write that there ought to be no commanders or officers because all are equal in Christ, therefore, no masters nor officers, no laws nor orders, no corrections nor punishments; I say, I never denied, but in such cases, whatever is pretended, the commander or commanders may judge, resist, compel, and punish such transgressors, according to their deserts and merits. This, if seriously and honestly minded, may, if it so please the Father of lights, let in some light to such as willingly shut not their eyes."

Williams took the broad ground from which

he never retreated during his whole career, that no man can be held responsible to his fellow man for his religious belief, so long as he respects the equal rights of his fellow men. With equal fervor he maintained that the civil magistrate could deal only with civil things. In his "Bloudy Tenent," in answer to John Cotton, the Puritan, he maintained that the sovereign power of all civil authority is founded in the consent of the people.

The ideals and purposes of Roger Williams were wrought out in his experiment in Rhode Island, and he demonstrated to all the world that a government based upon individual initiative and equal opportunity and the free exercise of the conscience in religious matters, was far superior to any government that regimented and prescribed all things to all men. He demonstrated beyond the shadow of a doubt that the happiest, most peaceful and prosperous people are those who live under a government in which the people are ruled by the least legislation necessary. Many believed in religious liberty, but only for themselves. Some believed in the freedom of conscience for others, but the high honor was reserved for Roger Williams to establish the first government upon the consent of the governed, where all men of every religious persuasion and of no religion, and the inalienable rights of the individual, should enjoy the equal protection of the law. Truly did the great American historian, George Bancroft, say of him:

"He was the first person in modern Christendom to assert in its plenitude the doctrine of the liberty of conscience—the equality of opinions before the law. . . . Williams would permit persecution of no opinion, of no religion, leaving heresy unharmed by law, and orthodoxy unprotected by the terrors of penal statutes. . . .

"We praise the man who first analyzed the air, or resolved water into its elements, or drew the lightning from the clouds; even though the discoveries may have been as much the fruits of time as of genius. A moral principle has a much wider and nearer influence on human happiness; nor can any discovery of truth be of more direct benefit to society, than that which establishes a perpetual religious peace, and spreads tranquillity through every community and every bosom.

"If Copernicus is held in perpetual reverence, because, on his deathbed, he published to the world that the sun is the center of our system; if the name of Kepler is preserved in the annals of human excellence for his sagacity in detecting the laws of the planetary motion; if the genius of Newton has been almost adored for dissecting a ray of light and weighing heavenly bodies as in a balance—let there be for the name of Roger Williams at least some humble place among those who have advanced moral science, and made themselves the benefactors of mankind."—"*History of the United States,*" *Vol. I, pp. 282, 283.*

While the people of Rhode Island did not always adhere strictly to the ideals of Roger Williams after he passed off the stage of action, yet they were exceedingly jealous for the preservation of their peculiar institutions of religious liberty and freedom of conscience which the founder of Rhode Island had bequeathed to them as their peculiar heritage. When the Constitutional Convention in Philadelphia, in 1787, left the question of the establishment of a state church and of religious liberty untouched and undecided in the Constitution which it submitted to the people for ratification, the people of Rhode Island deliberately refused to ratify the Constitution, and served notice to the Federal Government that they would never ratify it unless and until a Bill of Rights was added that guaranteed absolute separation of church and state, the noninterference of the Federal Government in religious matters, and the unmolested and free exercise of the conscience of the individual in religious concerns.

Three years passed by, and still Rhode Island held out against ratification after all the other States had ratified and were operating under the Constitution. Finally Congress threatened the little colony. Bills of coercion were introduced into Congress and discussed. Still Rhode Island said no. The people of Rhode Island repeated their request for constitutional safeguards in favor of religious liberty and the inalienable rights of all men.

A Missionary to the Indians

When Roger Williams was banished the first time from the Salem pastorate, he became a teacher and missionary to the Indians. He taught them that Christianity was a religion of love and peace to all men and that God and Christ were no respecters of persons. All were equal before God. He translated portions of the Gospels into the language of the Indians. He spent two years at Plymouth, and made many friends, not only among the Pilgrims, but among the Indians, and the Indian chiefs often submitted their troubles to Mr. Williams for equitable adjustment and arbitration. Thus he prevented a number of imminent hostilities among the Indians, and won many to the faith of Christianity. In the summer of 1633 a second call brought him again to the pastorate of the Salem church.

Steps were taken by the other States to boycott and isolate Rhode Island to compel her to come into the Union by ratifying the Constitution. Even Washington became irked and impatient at Rhode Island's delay. Hamilton thought she ought to be coerced to ratify. Congress proposed by legislation and by threat of force to bring her into line with the rest of the States. But Rhode Island stood as firm as Roger Williams used to stand in "the rockie strength" of his convictions. She was ready to arm herself, "one man against sixty."

At this critical moment James Madison and Thomas Jefferson, who had been ardent disciples of Roger Williams' principles, came to the rescue. Thomas Jefferson had expressed the wish and hope that some of the States would refuse to ratify the Constitution until proper guaranties of human rights and religious freedom had been annexed. Jefferson said, "By the Constitution you have made, you have protected the government from the people, but what have you done to protect the people from the government?"

Madison and Jefferson finally persuaded President Washington to untie the Gordian knot by recommending the annexation of a Bill of Rights to the Constitution. Washington agreed and suggested that Madison become a candidate for the House of Representatives in Congress, so that he could engineer through Congress the adoption of the recommendation for the Bill of Rights. Madi-

son was elected from Virginia upon the pledge that
he would secure, if elected, the passage of a resolu-
tion to add ten amendments to the Constitution
known as "the Bill of Rights," guaranteeing religious liberty as one of the fundamentals of a free
people.

Because of this guaranty and pledge given to
them, the people of Rhode Island ratified the Constitution of the United States on May 29, 1790, and
entered the sisterhood of the thirteen original
States which completed the union of the United
States of America. Yet Rhode Island would not
ratify without sending with her certificate of ratification the following request and admonition:

"That religion, or the duty which we owe to
our Creator, and the manner of discharging it,
can be directed only by reason and conviction, and
not by force or violence, and therefore, all men
have an equal, natural and unalienable right to the
free exercise of religion, according to the dictates
of conscience, and that no particular religious sect
or society ought to be favoured, or established by
law in preference to others."

Seventeen days after the ratification of the Constitution by Rhode Island, June 15, 1790, the great
Bill of Rights, guaranteeing religious liberty in
the First Amendment of the Constitution, together
with other inalienable rights, was adopted and
placed in the Constitution as the sheet anchor of
American liberties. Thus the great principle of

religious liberty and the separation of church and state, as well as the principle that civil government should function "in civil things only," which Roger Williams established in the founding of Rhode Island in 1636, became an established principle in the founding of the Federal Government under the Constitution of the United States, as the result of the persistent refusal of the followers of Roger Williams to ratify the Constitution, until assured of religious freedom under the Constitution. Indirectly, (Roger Williams became the builder, through the adoption of his ideals, of the greatest republic in the world.)

(If a man's ideals and work survive him and continue to bring forth a harvest of precious fruit in blessings upon humanity, he is a truly great man.) The best way to judge this man is by the contrast between the Puritan scheme of government and the Rhode Island experiment. The Puritans in Massachusetts and Connecticut established their government upon the theory: "Subjection in the Lord ought to be yielded to the magistrates in all lawful things commanded by them for conscience' sake;" and "matters of faith and worship, . . . or such erroneous opinions or practices, as either in their own nature, or in the manner of publishing and maintaining them, are destructive to the external peace and order which Christ has established in the church, . . . may be lawfully called to account, and proceeded against by the censures of the church and by *the power of the civil magistrate.*" The Puritans, in prescribing the duties of the civil magistrate, laid down the following rule:

"It is his duty to take order, that unity and peace be preserved in the church, that the truth of God be kept pure and entire, that all blasphemies and heresies be suppressed, all corruptions and abuses in worship and discipline be prevented or reformed, and all the ordinances of God duly settled, administered, and observed."—*Westminster Confession, 1648, Chap. XXIII, sec. 3.*

On this hypothesis of government, the Puritans proceeded to unite the church and the state and to enforce every religious obligation, every divine ordinance, and religious custom and observance under the duress of civil magistrate and the penalties of the criminal codes. Everybody was compelled to support the established church by the payment of his tithes, whether he was a member of the church or not. All parents, whether members of the established church or not, had to have their infants officially sprinkled, or suffer punishment at the whipping post or by a fine. Everybody had to attend "divine services on Sunday," whether a professor of religion or not, or pay a fine of ten shillings. All labor and secular business of every kind, except works of necessity and charity, were prohibited on Sunday, under the penalty of the whipping post or fines and imprisonment. One of the Sunday laws read as follows:

"Whosoever shall profane the Lord's day, or
any part of it, either by sinful servile work, or by
unlawful sport, recreation, or otherwise, whether
willfully, or in a careless neglect, shall be duly
punished by fine, imprisonment, or corporally. . .
But if the court, upon examination, . . . find that
the sin was proudly, presumptuously, and with a
high hand committed against the known command
and authority of the blessed God, such a person
therein despising and reproaching the Lord, shall
be put to death."

Both Massachusetts and Connecticut, under the
Puritan regime, enacted more than two hundred
fifty separate and distinct compulsory Sunday-
observance regulations, many of which are still
existent upon the statute books of the States which
comprised the thirteen original colonies.

Roger Williams would have none of these religious regulations upon the civil statute books of
Rhode Island. That State never had a compulsory
Sunday-observance law upon its statute books, nor
any religious obligation enforced under the penal
codes, while Roger Williams had a controlling
voice in affairs. Nor did he believe the church or
any of its schools in which religious education was
imparted, should receive financial aid from the
general tax fund. He was just as much opposed to
subsidizing the religious teacher as he was to paying
the clergy from the general tax fund of all the
people. His reasons for opposing a state subsidy

to religious institutions were sound. It is unjust to tax an unbeliever to support the teaching of religion. State subsidy for the support of religion means state control of religion. To the Puritan clergy this new doctrine was "heresy," and to the Puritan magistrate it was "sedition."

When Roger Williams struck a blow at the authority of the civil officers to interfere with church matters and to punish offenses against God and religion, he was condemned and "expelled" by the General Court for "new and dangerous opinions against the authority of the magistrates." He told them that he would "never refuse to obey them in purely civil matters." His persecutors informed him that they were not punishing him "for his religion," but for "sedition," and "disturbance of the public peace," and "jeopardizing the public good."

This was the same pretext upon which the pagan rulers of Rome burned the early Christians at the stake. It was this same kind of sophistry that the Jewish ruler invoked when he justified the crucifixion of Christ, saying "that it was expedient that one man should die for the people." Under a religion established by law, irrespective of its kind, whether pagan, Jewish, or Christian, religious persecution is inevitable and religious liberty impossible. As the Jewish hierarchy thought they would put an end to Christ by crucifying Him, so the Puritan hierarchy thought they would put an end to the alleged "dangerous and damnable heresies" taught by Roger Williams by sending him into exile. The Puritans banished him to the wilderness to perish, but Providence watched over him, protected and nurtured him, and gave him the courage of a hero and the spirit of a martyr. God had brought him into the world for such a time and such a mission as this. Persecuted in the Old World from his youth and banished in the New, he was led forth by Providence to a new and goodly land to found an asylum for the oppressed children of God, where the wicked should cease from troubling them.

"Careless seems the great Avenger; history's pages but record
  One death grapple in the darkness 'twixt old systems and the
      Word;
  Truth forever on the scaffold, wrong forever on the throne—
  Yet that scaffold sways the future, and, behind the dim un-
      known,
  Standeth God within the shadow, keeping watch above His
      own."